THE

FLAWLESS

MIRROR

THE

FLAWLESS

MIRROR

Kamala

*"The Divinity has not a place
on earth more allied to His nature
than a pure and holy soul."*

—Demophilus

Hardcover:

First printing, June 1964

Second printing, December 1964

Third printing, May 1975

Fourth printing, October 1979

Fifth printing, August 1987

Softcover:

Sixth printing, April 1993

© Copyright 1964 by

Kamala

© Copyright renewed 1992 by

Kamala

Distributed by

Crystal Clarity, Publishers
14618 Tyler Foote Road
Nevada City, CA 95959
1-800-424-1055

This book is Dedicated

To each Reader

I pray that Paramhansa Yogananda's words
will "light candles of wisdom" along your way,
and bring dulcet reminders of God to your heart.

I wish to express my appreciation to Bonnie B. Reed for her valued help in editing this book.

Contents

"The One Ocean of Spirit is hidden beneath the waves of finite forms."

—Paramhansa Yogananda

Paramhansa Yogananda

Foreword

"Introspection is a wonderful mirror,
but greater than that is to see your image
in the flawless mirror of a wise man's mind."
—Paramhansa Yogananda, *The Master Said*

ASSOCIATION with my Guru, Paramhansa Yogananda, over a period of 27 years, during long and shorter intervals, in various locations and under differing circumstances, is recorded here, knowing the hunger of devotees for words about their Preceptor.

I have been asked so often: "Tell about your days with Master." This is what I have endeavored to do. These pages include only that which touches directly upon my own discipleship and privileged hours with him. It is possible that some passage or pictured scene will give insight into the eternal quality of the Guru's relationship with the disciple. May this glimpse bless, as all who touched his life have been blessed.

Paramhansa Yogananda
Spiritual Emissary

CHAPTER 1

Enlightened Savant

THERE are crossroads in life which change the entire direction of travel. This was the hour of seeing my Guru. His precepts were to highlight my journey upon a way that led heart and thoughts Godward.

On the evening of January 13, 1925—eventful date—the Philharmonic Auditorium in Los Angeles was full to its 3000 capacity. The lines of people had queued around the building for great distances waiting for the doors to open; by 7 p.m. there was no more seating space for the hundreds who were still there. This was repeated each evening for many weeks. All had gathered to hear a certain emissary from India. From that land where Sages have been nurtured, we were to know one of her most illumined.

Swami Yogananda came upon the platform, his orange robe identifying him with an ancient order of renunciates. My spontaneous first impression was youthfully expressed in my diary. "His smile is like the sunshine of a soul." It was joyous and conveyed a warmth that seemed to envelope everyone.

How did I happen to be present? My Mother saw the billboards with his picture. Her interest was based on respect for the teachings of India, and she was "seeking truth." I went with her and attended all of his lectures and a series of beginning, advanced, and super-advanced classes, which were filled with hundreds of enthusiastic students. In response to a request for volunteers, I served as an usher at the classes and lectures.

Was I seeking? Not knowingly, but when I saw him I thought, "Now I have found one who can answer any question I may ever want to ask." School study brought forth academic answers, but they lacked a depth—a dimension I sensed should be there. In church I had received Christian teachings without a Rosetta stone to translate them into Realization. In Swami Yogananda I found this wisdom.

Paramhansaji* gave specific methods of meditation. These enabled one to know *how* to delve within and follow the soul's pathway to the Infinite. The few simple Yogic techniques which he presented were essentially direct. They guided one without by-paths.

Swami's lectures were preceded by organ playing, and the "Song of India" often prefaced his appearance. Before his

---

*A title conferred upon him by his own Guru some years later and *thereafter* used in place of "Swami."

talks he would read a poem, sometimes from his book *Songs of the Soul*. His powerful declaration proclaiming the soul's continuing survival through aeons of time is imprinted in my memory.

He had a fund of enthralling and unforgettable stories, each conveying a spiritual precept. Many were garnered from his own experiences; some he had brought from India.

One night he mentioned that in his childhood he was extremely thin and that his present weight had come as a true blessing of healing from his Guru. He was well aware that saintliness in the Western World is usually associated with thinness, even to a point of emaciation. With his keen enjoyment of humor, he explained that in India it is desirable to be pleasingly plump, because a thin teacher is a walking advertisement of his scarcity of pupils!

On another evening, someone asked about his age. Spontaneous guesses ranged from sixteen years to several hundred. But he replied, with a smile, "I never tell my age." This left the question still open to speculation. No one, then, fully grasped that he did not measure life solely by his brief residence in the body, for spirit is ageless.

He welcomed everyone, after one lecture, to come and touch his arms, which he caused to vibrate with energy in the manner of an electric power machine. This was a recharging of the body through will and life-force—a beneficial way of exercise which he taught in his classes.

There were several physicians taking his courses. On one occasion he asked if any doctors were present who would like to observe control of heartbeat. They were very interested and went up. With one on each side of him, touching his pulse at each wrist, they reported different counts at the left and the right. Then he caused all pulse to cease entirely, as well as breath. They could detect neither.

One night Swami invited all of the men of the Los Angeles Police Force who were present at the doors of the auditorium to come forward to see if several would be able to push him off balance, or move him from the place he stood. A number of them responded and were surprised to find their greater weight was of no avail in their efforts to dislodge him.

I was to learn that such demonstrations were rarely given by him, for he sought to bring others to God through love for the Heavenly Father and not by display of phenomenal powers.

On the first evening we heard him speak, he talked about the Super-conscious mind, which he described as the spiritual mind. He called the sub-conscious mind an imitator which imprints and records all of our actions, thoughts, and experiences.

He spoke nearly every night, for many weeks, and his words possessed an oratory of a kind to rouse the listener from spiritual slumber. For those who tended to regard his personality, he said, "Do not think of Yogananda but of Him Who sent me." He also said, "Do not accept blindly what I say; practice and prove for yourselves from your own experience."

There were prayer services which included affirmations for mental, physical, and spiritual well-being. Everyone participated and Swami's prayers and powerful vibrations reinforced our own. After one of the meetings I wrote, "I went to the healing service today and at the last of the prayers a wonderful Wave came down and filled the room. It was a sensation like a great blessing."

References to his classes appear in my diary notes. A few are included here.

January 21. I practiced the exercises this morning. They make me feel strong and healthy. Swami spoke about "Using Cosmic Consciousness in Daily Life." This means being in touch with love, courage, tolerance, sympathy, and wisdom.

January 28. Tonight was a revelation to us, as we are learning to know God, and hear Him through Cosmic Sound. Swami knows the *laws* to contact God, and how happy we are to learn them.

January 30. Our lessons, and all Swami tells us, are of great value. He speaks from an inner fount of wisdom. Tonight ended this first course and I have enough to keep busy for the rest of my life.

February 13. In meditation today the most wonderful realization came over me—a great love for God, my Father, Whom I feel near me.

After only one month I felt this close, personal feeling for God, which I never before had experienced in this way. It confirmed that the meditation techniques enable one to draw close to God. Swami said, "One must know God to love Him. Then His Peace will come into your hearts."

On March 8th Swami told of his plans for the purchase of the Mt. Washington Hotel building and premises to be used for the Yogoda work.* This site was located in one of the residential areas of Los Angeles and, when finding this place

---

Yogoda designated his teachings—a name that was later changed to *Self-Realization Fellowship.* In India the original name of Yogoda Sat-Sanga continues to be used. In translation this means "that which imparts union (of the individual soul with God) through fellowship with truth."

which he had seen in earlier vision, he was especially pleased it was named after America's great Pioneer of Freedom.

Mt. Washington was acquired and became the permanent Yogoda (SRF) Headquarters. The grounds include many acres upon a hilltop, and from the building one looks upon rolling hills, and the distant sparkling lights of the city. The first meeting, held there, was on Easter—a Sunrise Service. Swami talked of Jesus, and of realizing the Consciousness of Christ in our hearts.

In the late spring and summer Swami spoke in various cities in California, including San Francisco. He had lectured there the previous year, and now again met with great responsiveness. He also traveled up the coast to fill return engagements in the states of Oregon and Washington. He had many students in Portland and Seattle awaiting him. In Spokane also, throughout his September visit, he found audiences nightly overflowing the capacity of the large lecture hall. In October he returned to Los Angeles to speak again at the Philharmonic Auditorium. I wrote in my diary, "My great teacher, Swami Yogananda, is back. He spoke on Yogoda, and the ways the Masters of India have achieved God-Realization."

We always brought friends with us to all of his lectures. Our enthusiasm was boundless. Mother and I were drawn by his great wisdom, serenity, and radiant spiritual force that one could feel. As I absorbed his teachings, I had not felt the added need to go to him for a personal interview as did many of the students. However, we were now going to be away, so I wished to speak with him. It was nine months since I had first attended his lectures in January, and this evening of October 13th would be my first conversation with him.

After his lecture I went backstage and saw him standing near the wings. I observed his gentle dignity and the reserve that was always natural with him. This teacher was revered in my mind and heart in a way that I could not describe, but I later learned that this is the feeling of a disciple for the Guru.

I went up to him and he greeted me. We talked for a little while and he told me he was also leaving very soon to speak in other states.* With him was the newly arrived teacher for Mt. Washington and he introduced us. Swami said to come and see him again before we left.

His lecture on that evening had been a beautiful talk on living the life of Christ, Krishna, Buddha. He said that Christ came when love was needed, that Buddha brought spiritual determination, and Krishna emphasized wisdom-guided activity. His enlightening lecture, the next evening, was on

---

*His lectures for the following months were scheduled for Chicago, Rochester, Cleveland, Pittsburgh, and New York at Carnegie Hall.

"Quickening Human Evolution," and he described the help given through certain yoga techniques.

I received a blessing from my Guru on the following night. Swami spoke about his own great teacher, Sri Yukteswar. After the lecture I went to see him. He welcomed me and during our talk he said, "Always keep your dignity and remember your power of thought and will." As I was leaving I asked his blessing. He placed his hand on my head and prayed. At first, I felt inner stillness; then a sacred joy filled me as my spirit was lifted into an immense peacefulness.

CHAPTER 2

Treasured Friendship

SUNDAY services and weekly lectures were now held at the new Mt. Washington Headquarters. Mother and I attended regularly. In the summer of 1926 we went there to live and serve, at the invitation of the resident teacher who had been placed in charge by Swami Yogananda.

The building was scarcely occupied and we had our choice of dozens of rooms—all unfurnished at that time. We chose a suite on the second floor and had it painted; then sent for our own furniture. Mother donated monthly sums to cover our food and living expenses. She received the visitors who came from far and near and made them welcome until the teacher in charge could see them. Mother was a physician and her voluntary service was possible because she had recently retired from medical practice.

I found the stock room needed attention and at once began to bring order into it by working steadily each day. I also worked in the office answering some of the letters sent in by Yogoda students.

Swami Yogananda was lecturing throughout America most of the time but returned to California for extended periods. Each opportunity to see him, and the thoughts he expressed in my presence, left deep impressions. He was soon to be here for his summer vacation.

Many details of these days are recalled through diary notes. They leave a record that is factual and more dependable than memory. A fragment of a day may be viewed from some of the recollections, and I hope a kaleidoscope of such scenes will form a composite picture.

On August 18th we were happily busy at Mt. Washington with preparations for Swami's arrival. The next afternoon many students met him at the train and presented him with a beautiful bouquet of flowers. Mother and I were in the car with him as we rode back. He seemed immersed in God. Later he said to us: "Cultivate God's Friendship; meditate on Him and feel Him. Be a stubborn child and knock at the door until He opens it." In the evening he visited with us for a while and said that he was very pleased that we were there.

Swami had brought fresh mangoes with him from the East Coast. The next night we had mango ice cream, which he had planned as a surprise for everyone. He touched a blossom at the table, and remarked: "In the flowers we capture the beauty of God." He had Galli-Curci recordings and many

Swami Yogananda with Guests at Mt. Washington

spiritual songs from India which he played for us. He enjoyed listening to them and sharing them with us.

We attended a symphony concert with Swami and heard "Death and Transfiguration" by Strauss. We were at the Hollywood Bowl and Ralph Waldo Trine (author of *In Tune with the Infinite*) was there. Swami and he were acquainted. He, his wife, and son were invited to Mt. Washington for a luncheon the next day. I took pictures of them with Swami.

Those of us who were living at Mt. Washington, and other guests, were invited by Swami on a holiday excursion to Catalina Island. We were given nice rooms at the hotel and then went out to take drives around the island. We also had a picnic lunch. Afterward, several went in swimming, and a footrace followed. Five participated in the running contest. I noted that Swami's foot movements seemed to match the rapidity of pistons in a racing motor, and the long strides of the others were no match for him. He outdistanced even the nearest one by a whole block in a two-block race! Mother and I enjoyed watching this event.

The next morning we rode in motor boats for miles over the smooth waters, seeing many seals. Later we took a special trip in the glass-bottom boat. It was exquisite. We saw beautiful and colorful gardens under the clear water. That evening, on another trip, the flying fish were bright flashes of silver

Mother and I with Master in Motor Boat

leaping out of the water, even into our boat. We found so much of interest to see and do in the happy days spent there. Swami was a wonderful host to all.

When we returned to the mainland, Swami accepted our invitation to stop at our cottage in nearby Manhattan Beach. On the way we marketed and later he cooked a meal of East Indian food that was relished by everyone. Friends of ours came by to see us, and Swami delighted their two small children with some games which he taught them to play. Then afterward, we all walked to the beach, where he and one of his guests went in swimming.

Later in the afternoon Swami read a few stanzas to us from a book of poetry that was at the cottage; then he became very still. After a silence his eyes filled with tears of devotion. He said, "Oh, Brahma is so good to me! There is a current surging within me and through my whole body. Such bliss!" Hours later, when we meditated, I had a spiritual experience. Of this I wrote, "It is just the beginning. I can't describe the joy."

It was an unexpected happiness to have Swami come to our home, and was the beginning of a time that allowed friendship to grow and deepen with the blessing of daily association with him.

We remained at Manhattan Beach for a few days, then drove with Swami and guests to Santa Barbara. It was his first visit to our home there. On that evening, following a conversation about the plays of Shakespeare, Swami delighted us with a dramatic portrayal of Anthony's famous oration from "Julius Caesar." He gave the spontaneous reading from flawless memory. It took place by candle light since the electricity was not on then.* A little later Shakespeare's strains, and all earthly drama, were forgotten as we turned mind and heart to meditation.

Afterward as we sat looking out into the star-lit sky, Swami told of the joy he felt in God.† He then spoke poetically, saying the Day and the Night were talking together in friendliness, and yet each wished the other to withdraw! The Day longed to reveal the beauties of the world; the Night felt the soft mantle of darkness brought serenity to mankind.

His words became a poem, created at that moment, wherein he related a search in the cosmos for the Infinite One. He asked of star and cloud: "Tell me, in stillness, whom do you see? Is it He Who within me thrilled me with an invisible touch and quickly fled unseen?" He inquired of all Nature: "Have you seen God's hidden Presence?"

We each felt the inspiration of these days. They seemed to pass so quickly! Swami always radiated an aura of peace; one

---

*Mother had recently built this house, but we had gone to Mt. Washington instead of occupying it.

†He described this as Nirbikalpa Samadhi: a state of Bliss-consciousness in God that remains constant even while engaged in outer activities.

of quiet happiness.* When we returned to Manhattan Beach he gave me an autograph album. These are the thoughts he inscribed:

> There is an Invisible Cord that binds the East and the West and all strangers. We are all strangers and there are no strangers since we are all of our one Father, God. Worship Him as Bliss, the most interesting thing within you.
>
> May He Whom I feel in the cool touch of the breeze, and watch wrestling in the ocean waves, and hear in the sea roar, and see emerging from the opening petaled-gate of flowers, be yours always in reality.
>
> Wherever in this house I have prayed I leave an everlasting altar of devotion built in the Invisible Ether, wherein ye shall find Him always. In the self-same places quickly delve deep within yourself with reverence and steady concentration and ye shall find that secret altar.
>
> Swami Yogananda

When we were again at Mt. Washington, interviews and many matters concerning the organization kept Swami occupied much of the time, but there were always periods of meditation, meals shared, and quiet talks. One day he took

---

*It will be immensely difficult for all who know Paramhansa Yogananda through his *Autobiography* to realize that his book had not then been written. We grew to know many of his endearing qualities without the background insight given in his book.

Wherever in this house I have prayed I leave an everlasting altar of devotion built in the Invisible ether, wherein ye shall find Him always. In the self-same places quietly delve deep within yourself with reverence and steady concentration and ye shall find that secret altar.

Swami Yogananda

Aug 31ot Sep 1st 1926

Part of My Guru's Inscription in My Album

February 22, 1925. One of Swami's Class Series Which We Attended.
He is seated in front row.

us to see the motion picture "Mare Nostrum." He played tennis every day on the large court across the driveway. He also spent time with his writings, and gave talks at both the Sunday and mid-week services. He reminded devotees: "Deepen your love for God; have devotion above all. Keep your words kind and use not only the mind but the heart." He also said, "Calmness is one of the greatest attributes of the soul."

Mother and I were blessed to be with him one evening when his love for God was expressed in an outpouring of prayer, spoken softly to the Infinite. His rapt absorption and blissful countenance testified to the Divine response and bless-ing. Another disciple who was present was inspired to take his words in shorthand.* We seldom spoke through the hours. Once I asked, "What should children pray?" He replied, "There should be prayers for them." He then gave prayers that told in simple language of kindness, of consideration, and integrity. He expressed ways to bring the Presence of God close to children, that they perceive His love in parents and friends, His help through teachers, His beauty in nature; and Realize God within the Silence, as the peace and joy within their hearts. As the dawn was lighting the room, spread-ing a rose color over the sky, the Swami stood, gave each a blessing, and then departed to his rooms, leaving with us an unforgettable memory of those hours.

*These prayers, including the ones for children, appear in his book *Whispers from Eternity,* published in 1929.

Swami Yogananda, Mother, and I, at Mt. Washington, 1926

Swami returned to the beach cottage to spend some of the time remaining before his departure for the East Coast. He loved the simplicity of our small home near the sea. It afforded a view of the ocean and was within sound of the waters. There was also quietness, with no demands upon his time. He always meditated in the morning, free from interruptions. He was ready for his first daily swim around noon, and often returned to the surf again during the day.

At our evening worship he sang and played chants at the piano. These chants* included many he had composed, as well as others from India. Mother and I loved to listen to these devotional songs.

Swami liked to drive in the late afternoon or early evening. Sometimes we went to nearby Palos Verdes and stopped there to meditate, sitting on the ground upon the hillside overlooking the ocean. On warm summer days the Pacific breeze was softly cool, and Swami was at once deeply absorbed in Samadhi at this beautiful spot. (Then unbuilt, it has since become a place of homesites.) The view from there included several beach towns along the coast, and at night each one appeared like a jewel-cluster with a necklace of lights joining them. We often drove over the hills and saw an occasional farm nestled in this seemingly remote area which was within a few minutes' drive from town or city.

*They appear in the song-book *Cosmic Chants.*

At mealtimes we had curries—very good and very hot! Swami liked to select the vegetables at the market and did most of the cooking. We helped with the preparations. He used a wide variety of vegetables, mushrooms, and sometimes channa (ricotta), which is a cheese that can be cooked and prepared in a number of ways. Rice was usually served plain with the curry, and dessert was fresh fruit.

Throughout Swami's busy years of lecturing and traveling, his diet consisted mainly of fruit and nuts, with rare opportunity to have home-prepared foods of his native land. He welcomed them and we shared his enjoyment of them.

One day when his departure date was near I asked what I should read. He suggested a few lines from the Bible and Bhagavad-Gita each day. He added: "Pray, meditate, and be sincere to yourself." He also said to me, "Loyalty to one's Preceptor is of great importance on the spiritual path." He gave me a specially made bracelet of silver, copper, and gold.* He felt it would benefit me to wear it.

We returned home to Mt. Washington from the beach cottage. Swami left shortly for a full booking of lectures in Eastern cities. At the train he gave a blessing to everyone and said to be kind, and live in harmony with one another.

I received the following letter from my Guru in November. He calls me Kamala, as he always did. It is the name he gave me, meaning Lotus. My given name is Mary.

*The purpose of this kind of armlet is given detailed explanation in the *Autobiography of a Yogi.*

Cincinnati, Ohio

Dear Kamala,

I will have to reply to you in telegram for I am just fighting for time. I was pleased to receive your letters. It seems just one day since I came here. I had great success.

I am glad you know of my sincerity. This is my richest treasure. (Regarding something I had written.)

In December I am so tied up that it is impossible to get away. I have to cover several places. I wish I were in Los Angeles to see you all. *Prepare yourself for God's great work.*

Write me. I will be here up to the 28th of November.

With blessings always,

Swami Yogananda

This and other letters from my Guru appear as he wrote them except for the occasional omission of a few lines or a paragraph, in order to shorten, or because the message was confidential.

On December 24th we received a gift from Swami of some copper craft made in India, and on his Christmas card he told of his activities, and coming lectures in Washington, D.C. He also sent his blessings for our "greatest spiritual unfoldment."

Prior to our going to Mt. Washington I had had surgery for my knee and a condition still remained to be corrected. Swami refers to this in a letter he sent from Washington, D.C., in March (1927), wherein he wrote, "Let me know your Doctor's decision. My blessings and prayers will protect you always."

An operation was scheduled for me in July. I was to be in a cast for some time afterward, so Mother and I returned to the beach cottage for this period. I wrote Swami to ask if he would be coming to the West Coast during the summer and expressed the hope that he would visit us then. He sent a reply from Buffalo, New York, in June.

Dear Kamala,

I do not know whether I will be in Los Angeles or not. If I go there I shall certainly be delighted to accept your and your Mother's hospitality, as the last time, which was so much appreciated.

With blessings to you and your Mother,

Swami Yogananda

CHAPTER 3

Honored Guest

IT was in midsummer when there was a knock at our door and Swami, smiling, was there. He had come to California for his vacation, arriving at Manhattan Beach in July (1927). We felt blessed that he was with us. Mother and I were aware of his great spiritual stature, yet his simplicity of manner allowed our very special respect for him to blend naturally with the friendship he gave us. He brought an atmosphere of joyousness.

During his visit, Mother and I motored with him to Santa Barbara and stayed at our home there. The town had a very leisurely feeling at that time; no one ever seemed in a hurry, which gave a sense of tranquility that we liked. The days were lovely and warm. Swami swam at the beach. We went on some of the nearby scenic drives, which were very beautiful and were settings for spiritual inspiration.

One afternoon while driving, my Guru went into a state of Samadhi. He was outwardly still, inwardly absorbed in God—his consciousness completely interiorized. I was aware of this and when the car arrived at the house, and Mother and the chauffeur went indoors, I hesitated, not knowing if he wished anyone to remain, or to be alone. So I stayed for a little while, very quiet, and then went inside. He came in later. I realized, some time after, that when he entered into a state of deep communion, a disciple was privileged to remain and meditate with him, and receive the blessing of being near.

He brought with him a harmonium—an Indian instrument with organ tones and a piano-like keyboard. He used it to accompany his chanting at our evening meditations.

Once we drove to Pismo Beach, many miles up the coast, and had dinner there. We always found Swami dear to be with, and his sense of humor was of a kind that seemed to bubble over and everyone enjoyed things twice as much.

On our return drive to Manhattan Beach he told me that he had seen many of his past lives and from them he had learned that the soul would accept nothing for long that was not perfection. He said: "No human being can give the joy that God can give; go to God always; give Him your life."

During these summer days friends occasionally stopped by and met Swami. In all environments he was gracious and quiet in manner. Through this quietness he imparted a warmth and sweetness felt by all.

It was at this time that my Father first became acquainted with my Guru, and they spent time together in friendly visiting. My parents had separated when I was twelve. Neither one had remarried and they always remained friends with kindly feelings toward one another. My Father showed a lifelong concern for our well-being and was present in any emergency, giving comfort and efficient help. Very dear to me, he was keenly missed in my life after his passing some years later.

I asked Swami what I could do in addition to the Yogoda lessons which I followed. He told me, "Meditate longer, with greater intensity, for otherwise the mind only nibbles and no realization will come."

He suggested that I go on a specific type of diet for a time, which I did, benefitting tremendously in health and energy. He also penciled this list:

1. Meditation 2. Dignity 3. Perfect Cooperation

4. Diet 5. Giving no cause of criticism

6. "Make yourself better and serve to please."

7. Seclusion is the price of spiritual greatness.

Shortly afterward Swami left with his driver for Pismo Beach to meditate. The now-thriving little sea town was then mostly rolling sand dunes. He remained there a few days. When he returned, the chauffeur said to Mother in a perplexed tone: "I don't know what he was doing, but he just sat out there among the sand dunes, facing the ocean, and stayed there every day, all day long."

My Father, William James Buchanan

Swami returned after these days in God-communion with the effulgence of that time upon him, and as he came into the room I remained quiet, sensing his inner rapture. He spoke words to God, of me, precious and sacred; then said solemnly, "Only speak to me of God." In that vibrant bliss in which he had remained in unbroken communion, it would have been painful and restricting to turn his gaze from his absorption in the Infinite to any other topic.

One facet of his true saintliness lay in his willingness and ability to meet the noisy world of constant public life and cope with every duty and yet stay permanently in the sanctuary of inner beatitude. Here, now, he could roam in the Cosmic Vastness without even a part of his mind having to turn to the multitudinous affairs of daily life. As Jesus went to the mountain top to pray, my Guru had gone by the ocean to commune with the Heavenly Father.

A few days later Swami left California. He bade us goodbye and said he would keep us in his prayers. His fall itinerary included Minneapolis, St. Paul, and Philadelphia.

Mother and I drove to Mt. Washington for both the Sunday service and the mid-weekly lectures which were conducted by the leader in charge. Throughout the years we always attended regularly. The distance was 25 miles each way from the beach but since then has been shortened in time sense, by the freeways. Near the hilly Mt. Washington area, one drove to Headquarters up a winding road with an unbelievable number of turns. Old pictures show this route which is seldom used now. The present avenue has few curves in comparison. However, I recall the old road with fond regard because we drove it so often, and when once on it we were then close to our destination.

Swami wrote to us about the special second anniversary dinner in October to commemorate the establishing of the Center at Mt. Washington. He would be unable to return for it but hoped that we would be present. At the banquet that night, the resident teacher invited Mother to speak. Mother asked me if I would give the address in her place. I spoke of our dearly loved founder of the Center: Swami Yogananda, who was with us in spirit on that night.

An Early View of Mt. Washington at Top of Winding Road

CHAPTER 4

Hospital Visits

ELEVEN months elapsed before my Guru returned to the West Coast. The two following diary excerpts preceded the days of Swami Yogananda's return to California for his 1928 summer vacation. I was hospitalized after recent surgery, and in a full body cast which remained on for seven months.

July 7. I thought of God and Omnipresence as I went under anesthesia, but in the following days I could not meditate at all because of pain, except for one wonderful experience a few mornings later. The nurse was busy in my room and Mother was sitting nearby. I was awake but closed my eyes and was instantly absorbed within, entirely free of the world. It came suddenly! I was out of pain; the body was forgotten in the feeling of peace, great space, and God. I was aware of being a part of Him. I learned the great difference between ordinary consciousness and that Eternal, Timeless kind.

July 12. Mother is over every day nearly all day. I have a little room to myself. Everyone is kind. I have continual pain

My Mother, Dr. Frances Grant Buchanan

which I can expect for a few days. Doctor comes in every day for a few minutes. Mother's being here helps me to feel better—her love and tenderness mean so much.

The fact that Mother was a physician gave her the privilege to be at the hospital a great deal of the time.*

One day when Mother came into the room I noticed her expression of delight. Someone was with her and she knew I would be joyous. My Guru was here! It is hard to describe the impact of his presence then and always when I saw him. Greetings were outwardly quiet; only a few words spoken but heart and spirit were shining. I felt the radiance which his ever-present bliss state imparted. Diary notations recall some of his visits.

July 16. Swami Yogananda came to the hospital to see me. He stayed for an hour. He and his driver have been at our beach cottage since early today.

July 17. Swami and Mother came for a little while, bringing me some English toffee. After they left I broke into tears, missing them. Oh where is my yoga teaching? If I only could meditate more.

---

*Mother received her degree from the Denver and Gross College of Medicine of the University of Denver a few years after the turn of the century. She later went to Chicago to take added courses on Ear, Nose, and Throat, with special work in Ophthalmology. Her field of service was that of a general M.D., and she practiced in Colorado, Utah, and in California, where she was a charter member of the Los Angeles Branch of the American Medical Women's Association.

July 19. Swami brought me a delicious curry dinner he had cooked at the cottage. He ate with me and stayed for a while afterward. The pain is less and I can meditate better now.

July 21. I am so happy tonight; Swami Yogananda was here a couple of hours. He told me he has seen his Mother several times since her death. He also talked about many spiritual things.

July 24. Swami spoke about the happiness he saw among the children at this hospital. While we were visiting he said, "I see marriage for you." He explained certain conditions that I would find if I were to marry. (Later, this came true exactly as he described.)

July 26. Swami had dinner with me this evening. He told me about the talk he had given Sunday on "Is This Life a Dream?" Later he wrote two wonderful poems and then read them to me. They touched my heart. I felt so keenly his holiness.

Meals with my loved Guru can be visualized. His plate was placed on a small table; my tray was beside me as I was encased in a cast and in traction. How wonderfully kind he was to prepare the food and bring it. He knew the happiness that these hours with him gave to me.

Mother was staying in Los Angeles to be near me. Swami included her in many of his holiday plans. He and his driver remained at our beach cottage for much of his vacation time.

July 27. Swami and Mother came at noon to see my Doctor, who took them through the hospital and the grounds. He is Dr. C.L. Lowman, founder of this Children's Orthopaedic Hospital. Swami said that Doctor is doing a Christ-like work. (He was named "Doctor of the Century," in 1971.)

July 28. Wonderful visit with Swami. He told me that God plans everything so wonderfully when we love Him, and have our hearts in Him as we serve in His work. He also told me about the Fair that he and Mother attended yesterday at Long Beach.

Mother and Swami drove to Santa Barbara for the Spanish Fiesta. This yearly event is a colorful revival of early California. The costumes, songs, and dances, the magnificent palomino horses on parade, the slow-moving carriages, with members of the old Spanish families—all is festive, yet it retains the dignity of the "don" and "doña" of another generation.

August 3. Swami brought me a gift from the Fiesta. It is a silver disc that opens and closes without any outside hinges. The craftsmanship is remarkable. There is a place for a small photo inside. Mother said when Swami saw it he was quite fascinated with the skill required to make it. So dear of him to bring it to me.

August 5. Tonight when Swami was here he told me that he is leaving to lecture in Boston, and to fill other speaking engagements. I will miss him but his blessings will continue to be with me.

I have known God's healing to reach many persons through the channel of my enlightened Guru. However, I never sought nor asked any kind of physical healing because of a request I had made to God. I had asked God to bring all of my karmic debts into *this* lifetime so that I might pay them and be free of them. I may have invited much, considering our many past lives!

Once, before making this request, I had an instantaneous healing when I was 19, following the prayers of my Mother. I was very ill and Mother sat beside my bed in the hospital room. I did not know until afterward that she was then praying, and had been, that healing would come to me as it had once come miraculously to her. She prayed because I had been very ill for several days. I had spent this day in silence thinking of the Star of Light, trying to be still. In the early evening I suddenly felt the presence of a Great Soul in the room. I said to my Mother, "There is a Master here."* He remained at the foot of my bed for several minutes, and before he left, his benedictions brought complete release

*In later vision I learned this was Sri Yukteswar.

from my suffering. Mother's prayers were answered. I was healed.

It may be relevant to speak of karma, and of my early belief and acceptance of karma as a *just* law of life. God does not blueprint our destinies; if He did we would be automatons. Our own strongly-developed tendencies, and desires, tend to direct our choices of action; these actions blueprint our lives through their resultant effects. Karma places the responsibility of our actions upon ourselves. The law of cause and effect, called karma, carries through from one incarnation to another, giving a long span of time for the maturing or fulfilling of karma in a circumstance or environment that is propitious.

All phases of our lives, not only the physical, are touched upon by the law of cause and effect, and all actions today are being woven into the pattern of tomorrow. If we rightly change, our healings are permanent, otherwise they are a respite. Often medical science works with nature to heal in "time" while one may learn the lesson and pay the debt. Instantaneous healings, through science and prayer, work in accord with karma. When a Master bestows healing, it is only with God's Sanction.

I believed that if I had sown a field with many weeds, I was reaping what I had planted. But I recognized the healing power of prayer, love, and deep meditation to be bright forces that can help change the karmic design in our lives.

Some good karma blossomed for me, too! I had the great love and kindness that surrounded me, and my Guru's continued guidance and patience through my working out of karmic conditions. I have always had his untiring help, that I change (myself) so that future plantings will harvest the right kind of crops!

In my worship, God was always Spirit, to be realized in Omnipresence and Light. To be in this Light, to feel Omnipresence in Spirit: these were my longings. God as Spirit was the God I loved and adored. My wording of "He" is from the term given by Jesus in the relationship of child to "Our Father," our Creator. I felt God as Spirit to be "nearer than thinking and breathing" in Bliss, Intelligence, and Divine Love, and ever-present for each one to realize through attunement. That there might be any more personal aspect of God than this puzzled me. Thus, it was during one of the many times that my Guru came to see me at the hospital that I asked him: "Is God Personal or Impersonal?"

Master wrote his reply to my question and then read it to me. His beautiful answer is presented here. It was included in his book *Whispers from Eternity* when published later.

Thou art Impersonal, Invisible, Unseen, Formless, Omnipresent, yet frozen by my devotion I beheld Thee sometimes as Krishna, sometimes as Christ—personal, visible, imprisoned in the little space within the temple of my love.

O Spirit Invisible, just as Thou didst freeze Thy unseen Infinitude into the seen Cosmic Finitude, so do Thou appear unto me visible and living that I may serve Thee. I want to see Thee as the Ocean of Life with and without the ripples of finite creation.

With blessings,

Swami Yogananda

Thou art Impersonal, Invisible Unseen formless, omnipresent, yet frozen by my devotion I beheld Thee sometimes as Krishna sometimes as Christ — Personal visible imprisoned in the little space within the temple of my love. O Invisible Thou didst freeze Thyself Thy unseen Infinitude into the seen Cosmic Finitude So do Thou appear unto me, visible & living. I want that I may serve Thee to see Thee as the ocean of life with and without the ripples of finite creation.

with blessings Swami Yogananda

My Guru's Reply to My Question: "Is God Personal or Impersonal?"

CHAPTER 5

Yoga Sweeps the Nation

A letter from my Guru reached us in May (1929) from New York. In it he spoke of his plans for the summer. "I am going to Mexico, starting on the 23rd of May, and then will visit Los Angeles for a short while."

He traveled to many parts of Mexico and while there he met the President of that country, Mr. Portes Gil, through the courtesy of the British Legation.

Swami always showed enthusiasm for the beauties of nature in all lands. He had marveled at the wonders of Yellowstone National Park, at the august splendor of Alaska, the breath-taking Himalayas, and the grandeur of Pike's Peak in Colorado, to mention but a few. In Mexico he was delighted by many places, and he included Lake Chapala and Xochimilco as among the most beautiful spots on earth that he had seen.

His vacation was also a time of deep meditation and during this period he composed the words and music for the chant "My Lord, I will be Thine Always."

Swami remained in Mexico much longer than he had originally planned. Mother and I were to be in Colorado by midsummer and wrote asking if he would be able to come there en route. He replied that he could see us.

August 30, 1929

Dear Kamala,

At last I succeeded in squeezing some time. I am running one month and a half late in my schedule.

I was very glad to hear from you. I will reach Colorado Springs on September 4th, Wednesday at 7:15 a.m. I hope to meet you at the station. Many things to tell you when I see you.

Unceasing blessings to you both,

Swami Yogananda

We eagerly awaited the hour he would be with us. A white dusting of snow touched the Rocky Mountains on the day Swami arrived. We met him and drove to our mountain cabin. We had guests staying with us and all were overjoyed to have this opportunity to be with him. It was a time of visiting and blessing, spent near the blazing log fire, necessitated indeed by the sudden departure of summer.

The next day we drove to Denver, where we were to remain overnight with friends whom we knew to be very interested in Swami's teachings. Master had graciously agreed to these plans, and found this couple had many questions to

Yogananda, Savant of the Swami Order

ask him. Recognizing their great sincerity, he asked if they would like to receive the lesson techniques. Their affirmative replies were given with happy anticipation. In the evening we all sat around a table and I recall we practiced the concentration and meditation methods as he explained them. He concluded with a blessing as he showed each one the inner spiritual light.

In the early hours of the following morning my Guru crossed the street into a park which faced the house. Everything was white with the early winter snow. There, beside a lovely pond of water, was a sheltered place for his devotions, and he meditated in this peaceful setting.

When we were leaving, our friends surprised and pleased him with a gift of a travel film of India taken by their son. Swami delighted in sharing the film. After he left Colorado he showed it in many cities during his lecture tour, and gave a special talk with it entitled "Visions of India."

When the time arrived for his departure, we were naturally reluctant to see him leave. It brought a lonely feeling when he boarded the train that carried him on his way, but we were glad he had been able to fit these days into his busy schedule.

It is difficult to convey the immense scope of his activities that commenced with his first cross-country lecture tour in 1924 and continued through the following years. Citizens of all professions endorsed his message: educators, lawyers, ministers, judges, editors, congressmen, and businessmen. He was invited to speak at universities, clubs, and churches of many denominations. He was guest of honor at banquets in many cities. This was all in addition to his scheduled lectures and classes.

Swami Yogananda was presented to the President of the United States, Mr. Calvin Coolidge, at the White House, by Mr. John Balfour of the British Embassy. The National League of American Pen Women in Washington, D.C. gave a reception in his honor.

"Never before has the National Capitol had such an outpouring of spiritual blessings, spread over all creed lines," commented Mr. Louis Van Norman, then Commercial Attaché of the U.S. Department of Commerce, and former editor of *The Nation's Business*.

Quotations from newspapers of that time show the great enthusiasm with which every part of America received him. In Washington, D.C., the *Washington Herald* stated: "Crowds are flocking to hear Swami Yogananda, distinguished East Indian Savant who is delivering a remarkable series of twelve public lectures at Washington Auditorium under the patronage of a committee of leading citizens of the National Capitol. During the past week his audiences each night have increased in numbers and enthusiasm until the capacity of the Auditorium (6000) is now being taxed to the uttermost."

The *Washington Post* said: "Swami has broken all records for sustained interest he has aroused in the thousands who have heard him speak."

When Swami spoke in Buffalo, the *Courier-Express* reported: "More than 3000 heard his first lecture. The audience overflowed the seating arrangements in the hall and many stood through the two hours."

The *Pittsburgh East Liberty Tribune* wrote: "Yogananda's class of almost 1,000 persons was a revelation to conservative Pittsburghers. . . . he has swept and startled Pittsburgh with his lessons and lectures on the use and conservation of life energy." The paper added that Swami was guest of Judge A. D. Brandon at the Morals Court. The Judge had wished to know the reaction of the Eastern mind to Western derelictions. He observed: "Swami's doctrine of all-pervading love, of ever reaching toward the light of understanding, covered even the miseries he saw in court."

The *Cincinnati Enquirer* said: "Swami Yogananda, Hindu educator, philosopher, and poet, discussed all questions with equal ease before a group of newspaper persons. His English was perfect and flowed with ease as he discussed religion, politics, mysticism, poetry, reformations, adding definitions occasionally that showed him to be no mean lexicographer. Every question brought forth an answer in which infinite thought was expressed. There is no sign of either youth or age in his face. Looking into eyes that could be said to be almost unsophisticated, one could see no trace of the flight of time over him."

The *Detroit Free Press* stated: "He has no creed in the manner of the sectarian. . . . He has modernized some of the most sacred practices of India. He is an ardent advocate of world peace and human brotherhood."

The *Los Angeles Times* wrote of Yogananda: "A Hindu invading the United States to bring God . . . in the midst of a Christian community, preaching the essence of Christian doctrine."

A bi-monthly magazine *East-West* was published regularly, officially representing the Yogoda work and keeping members informed of all activities. It presented topics of spiritual value. The first issue was printed in November 1925 and contained an account of Swami's work in India and America.

This publication has continued for half a century, although, for many years, printed under the title of *Self-Realization Magazine.**

*Designated *SRF Magazine* in further references in these pages.

*A drawing of the SRF Lotus Symbol. This is described on the
following page. The dark wings represent eyebrows; between them,
above, is the Star of Light within the single eye.*

The symbol used in all SRF literature portrays a lotus. Superimposed on this is a golden disk which contains a deep blue center, and within this is a silver star of light. This is a description of the "single eye" of meditation that is within everyone, and mentioned by Christ when he said: "If therefore thine eye be single, thy whole body shall be full of light." (Matthew 6:22)

The Yogoda Sat-Sanga activities are widespread in India, with many YSS Ashrams in various parts of the country. Swami also established residential schools there, to give children a rounded education. Yoga training in concentration, meditation, re-energizing exercises, and moral values are taught together with the curriculum of basic school studies.

Swami Yogananda came to the United States in 1920 as a delegate from India to the Congress of Religious Liberals in Boston. At this assembly he spoke on "The Science of Religion"—a talk later elaborated into his book by that title. He first established a Center in Boston, and remained there, teaching, four years. It was on his trip to the West Coast in 1924, and in the ensuing years, that he carried the message of practical Yoga across America.

Master came to this Rocky Mountain area when he visited us in Colorado in the summer of 1929.

CHAPTER 6

Priceless Precepts

SWAMI returned to Los Angeles in November (1929), where he lectured and remained for a time at Mt. Washington. Mother and I were again in California and attended his lectures. We were also present at the meditations and festivities of Christmas, where Swami was host to the gathering of resident disciples and guests.

This season prefaced the advent of my Guru's new book, *Whispers from Eternity*. The Christmas card which I received from him was inscribed:

To Kamala, For undying devotion to God and Yogoda. Unceasing blessings. A *Whispers from Eternity* is soon coming to you, to whisper eternally God to you.

Swami Yogananda

His words voiced truth, as always. These prayers have inspiringly lifted my thoughts to God. Their guiding precepts, expressed in poetic imagery, are aflame with devotional feeling for the Infinite.

Serenity—Reflection of Inner Peace

His book *Whispers from Eternity* reflects God's Whispers in his soul.

On Mother's Christmas card he also penned a special greeting and mentioned the volume which she would receive. When our copies arrived, both were autographed and included a message for each. On my copy he had written:

> To Kamala, Look steadily at the Polestar of His Presence. He knows you are trying to reach Him, only keep trying. Once you convince Him, you will be there. Without side-tracks, let's hurry to His place.
>
> Swami Yogananda

In January (1930), Swami was invited to give the main address at the dedication of the Sikh Temple in Stockton, California. There were several persons from Mt. Washington who were going to accompany him, and my Mother drove some of them in our car.

When we arrived at the Temple, Swami left his car and mingled with the men on the grounds surrounding the new edifice. A lively discussion was taking place. The Sikh members (men) debated whether to introduce chairs into the Temple, or to sit on the carpeted floor: the new versus the old. The chairs won! The services were to be held that evening and Swami's talk was to be given in his native language.

When I went into the Temple that night with our group, I did not know the name of Singh is given to every member of the Sikh faith. Before the ceremony commenced, Mr. Singh, who had driven up with us, was wanted by Swami. Everyone was seated and I was sent to ask him to come to the back of the hall. I started down the aisle and when I saw him a few rows beyond, I called in an audible whisper, "Mr. Singh." As I did so, every head in the spacious auditorium turned around! I will refrain from describing my feelings, but "our" Mr. Singh responded by coming to the back of the room.

We remained overnight in Stockton. On our return trip an incident took place that revealed my Guru's perception. It was quite heart-clutching when I learned all of the story. In our car Mother and others alternated at the wheel. I rode with Swami in his car. As we reached the old winding Ridge Route beyond Bakersfield, snow was falling and much of it was turning to ice. It was here that Swami asked that his car be stopped, and that Mother's car be signaled to stop. He cautioned Mother and the others to drive very, very carefully. To me he said, "I see some danger." I had faith that his prayers would give Divine protection. I learned the import of the danger when Mother commented upon it by merest chance, long after. She told me that when they were driving over the slippery, steep mountain road, she spoke to the driver but he did not answer. He was asleep at the wheel! She took hold of it just in time.

One day Swami invited Mother and me to come to Mt. Washington to accompany him on a picnic, early the next morning. We were unavoidably detained at Manhattan Beach, causing us to arrive late, and we found him busy with organizational work, important matters that required his attention. Swami greeted us, then said, "You are late!" Mother replied that she was sorry, "But," she added, "I knew that no matter how late we were, we would still be early." He asked her to repeat her words, spoken so spontaneously, to be sure he heard correctly. Then his eyes filled with merriment, and he enjoyed repeating this ambiguous statement, chuckling appreciatively at the truth it contained. Delay was usual with him because of the many interruptions that prevented his getting away. On that particular day we left Mt. Washington hilltop with him at 6 p.m. for our picnic. This was one of the reasons why my Guru frequently returned to our beach cottage during vacations—to be away for a little while from the constant demands upon his time.

We rarely took pictures of Swami, since his life throughout the year was so full of activity that it seemed to us a courtesy not to ask him to pose. But I do not believe, as I think of it now, that he would have minded, and I love the few pictures which I do have. Several of them appear on these pages.

One day when we were at the beach cottage with Swami, I brought my notebook to him and asked if he would write in it. He nodded and reached for his pen. Momentarily he looked out over the blue water, and then he wrote:

Yonder ocean is immovable, not always within reach—so bathe in the Shoreless Sea which you carry within yourself, in the thrilling billows of ever-surging joy of God contact— whenever you desire, any time, anywhere.

I learned many precepts from my Guru by observation. I noted how he greeted people with a friendliness and warmth that divinely included everyone. His smile and expression showed equal regard for all. It became an object lesson to me when I observed others in the personal exchange of glances that suggests flirting. I realized that the magnetism in the eyes is a power that can mirror the ego by attracting attention to itself when used in this manner. But this magnetic power can be transformed into a glow of Godly feeling for all, when it mirrors the vast Soul, as in my Guru's example. The contrast was so marked I felt this was a precept to emulate if one was seriously seeking God.

Master gave practical help for the solution of problems in business and other fields of earning a livelihood. In the laws for success that he taught, he placed emphasis upon prayer, and upon understanding the magnetic influence of environment. Benefits are gained through association with others in their environment of success. This is also true spiritually. Swami spoke of the divine magnetic qualities of saintly lives, and of holy places that can strongly influence those who are responsive.

A Smiling Profile of My Guru

Master's words—"Company is stronger than will power"— were a startling thought to me! It caused me to observe myself over a long period of time before I realized fully this pragmatic truth. I noted that we acquire attitudes, ideas, manners of speech, habits, ideals, or lack of them, from those we see most often. It may be at once, or later, after they are away from our lives. But they leave their imprint. We absorb unconsciously and are influenced to a greater degree than we realize. Worldly companions draw the mind away from thoughts about God. Benefit is derived through good company. Master has written, "Environment is of supreme importance."

Swami said, "I use my sensitiveness only to absorb spirituality." I observed that he abided by this rare precept all through the years. How natural it is to react to negative moods, remarks, and attitudes of associates! He never did so, yet the doors of his responsiveness were open wide to anyone who showed sincere interest in things of the spirit. Once on the train, when he was sitting in a deep meditative state, the porter passed him many times, glancing wonderingly at him, and finally he stopped and said, "You look so peaceful sitting there." Swami replied, "I wish you could know what I feel." The man answered, "So do I." Master offered to show him how to find this peace in meditation. When the porter was free of duties he returned and Master taught him the lesson techniques.

Swami always acted with positive will; he did nothing half-heartedly. He said, "Exercise your will in every undertaking." His precepts describe blind will, thinking will, and Divine Will. I pondered the latter, seeking the meaning of God's Will in relation to my own, to know how to differentiate. Our Guru reminded us that God's Will is not separated from our own: "If our will is guided by wisdom, it is God's Will. If our will is guided by ego, it is without God's sanction. Do the best you know how. God wants from us the continuity of effort, and that we should not run away from our duties."

When Master said: "Concentrate on the similarities, not on the differences," he was speaking of nations, and of people in their many relationships: family, social, and business. I found this to be a key to establishing rapport with others. It dissolves critical attitudes, for differences separate people. We grow closer when we keep our attention upon the things we have in common.

Swami's use of devotional chants emphasized the blessings to be realized through this form of worship. Chanting helps one to become attuned to God. It can ease tensions and emotional disturbances, thus creating an inner stillness. As with affirmations, the vibratory power within certain words reaches deep into our consciousness, through repetition, and influences our daily affairs as well as our inner spiritual life.

At Mt. Washington one afternoon Swami had gone to the fourth-story open porch for a period of worship (a porch later enclosed), and when he came down into the foyer where several of us were present, he remarked that when meditating there was never need to be ostentatious by commenting upon it. He advised that one can say, simply, "I was a little busy."

My Guru told me, "Where others leave off, there I am just beginning." At times, when about to conclude my meditations, I recall his words, and continue; often to be blessed in measure not touched during the first part.

First efforts to become still are difficult for almost everyone. It is not easy to withdraw from customary identity with body and possessions, and attachment to each. We seldom know how to detach ourselves from our memories, from recollection of daily events, and from all mental, emotional, and physical restlessness. The concentration method of "Hong-Sau" that Master taught gives quietness to mind and body. Peace and many other blessings are found in this relaxed state: a stillness in which breath forgets its ceaseless movement. It is this Yoga lesson that has been of the greatest help to me. I believe it was my regular and prolonged practice of this important technique which opened the way for many of the blessings that I received from God and Guru. Consistent in daily practice, I added other times for this exercise, as when traveling or waiting for appointments, as it is not apparent to others as one sits quietly.

In meditation we seek to dwell in that pure Consciousness that remains unchanged through eternity. This Consciousness, alone, can know God. Avatars, dwelling in this illumined state, offer help to man. "Wisdom is implanted by the Guru," Master has said, "but the receptivity, and power of growth, must be supplied by the devotee."

We tend to remain in familiar paths of habit, tendency, and inclination, and follow round and round a known way—moving but not rising. A Guru's Precepts may be unfamiliar in ways of yoga practice and disciplines, but they lead upward where the soul sheds its transient trappings, and its limited allegiance to the senses, to reclaim the Freedom and Domain of Spirit.

My Guru taught that if we "Look to the Pure Beam of God's Presence" we will see that the shadowy substance of the moving pictures played on the screen of Life, all comes from the Projection Booth of God. Only by turning away from the scenes and *looking up* can one see the Beam projecting from the booth. It is in the Beam that we perceive Reality, and not in the movement upon the Screen.

CHAPTER 7

I Receive Kriya Initiation

NINETEEN thirty-three was a year in which I saw my Guru frequently, often daily, beginning with his unexpected visit to our home in Santa Barbara on January 4th. How wonderful to have this blessing! I was filled with the happiness his peaceful presence always brought.

He had come to give a series of public lectures and classes. I attended them and took his talks in shorthand. I had completed a 15-month secretarial course at the Santa Barbara Business College and this now proved of value in serving my Guru's work.*

My diary noted Swami was with us on January 5th. Many years later I learned this was his birthday. He made no mention of it, but he surely found our hearts full of happy rejoicing that he was there.

He was staying in a rented bungalow with his chauffeur and Ettie Bletch—a disciple from Mt. Washington who looked

---

*My academic studies were previously at the Santa Barbara State Teacher's College; later at the University of California in Los Angeles, and graduate courses at San Francisco State College.

Guru-Preceptor at the SRF Hermitage, Encinitas

after things for him during the lecture series. (She later accompanied him to India.) There was an earthquake in Los Angeles at that time, and he drove there at once to see that all was well at Mt. Washington and give them the comfort of his presence. Ettie invited me to stay with her. She was pleased that I could come and we became good friends. During this time I transcribed some of Swami's lectures on the typewriter from my shorthand notes.

When Swami returned, they came to our home for the remainder of his stay in Santa Barbara, while he conducted his classes. From the room which he occupied when he was there he could look upon the sunrise over the mirror-like bay, and at sunset he could view its last rays dipping into the ocean on the western horizon. This panoramic view included the long range of Santa Ynez Mountains. The trees of oak and eucalyptus on surrounding hills create a lovely setting for the city of Santa Barbara.

All of Master's lectures and lessons were given extemporaneously, but they followed a prearranged order of thought. When driving in the car with him one day, I asked if he would be giving two stories in his classes here, about a great yogi, King Janaka. They were favorites of mine that I had heard him tell, previously. He replied, "Well, they do not go with the lesson tonight, but I will if you wish them." In his considerate way, and to my delight, he told the stories and everyone enjoyed them.

The stories that Swami interspersed in his teachings could be heard many times with increased awareness of their instructive value. Many of them are now compiled within the SRF Praecepta Lessons. One story I enjoy gives amusing detail about a dangerous snake who reformed at the request of a saint, then nearly lost his life when it was no longer feared. When the poor bruised snake described its sad plight to the saint, the wise man replied, "I told you not to bite, but I didn't tell you not to hiss a little."

My Guru's way of relating stories was inimitable. Once in a while he used skillful pantomime to portray some attitude, as when he pictured this incident from his childhood remembrances. An adult in the family spent a great deal of time "in meditation" and as a result regarded herself as extremely pious. This opinion was not shared by all! Swami began to question the benefits of meditation when no benign influence was seen from her years of practice. Then he began to observe that throughout her daily retreat, numerous involvements with outer activities formed a regular pattern. During her many hours "in solitude" she kept an expertly watchful ear tuned in upon all that was going on in the household and frequently emerged to impart reprimand, instruction, or to include a list when someone was leaving for the store. Her outward interests left her exceedingly brief moments for spiritual communion. When Master perceived this conduct his faith in meditation was restored! It graphically illustrated for us the importance of inwardly-focused attention during meditation if benefits are to be derived.

One day Swami handed me an article to read which he had just written on "What Happens During Sleep?" We were at the beach and he walked up the coast on the sandy shore while I read. When he returned he asked, "Did you read it all? Tell me about it." I began to describe the thoughts it contained. When he was completely satisfied that I understood it, he nodded and said, "Yes, that's right."

I discovered Master's *Metaphysical Meditations* on the book table one evening. I became absorbed in it at once, reading the beautiful prayers and affirmations which channel the mind and heart to God.

One afternoon I was coming out of Trenwith's Department Store and Swami's car was standing there waiting for me. Mother had told him I was in town and he said he would drive me home. It was so unexpected to see him there! I felt as if the sun's radiance was lighting the whole area and surroundings with warmth. How can one describe this spiritual force?

Master was looking at a new edition of the *Rubaiyat* of Omar Khayyam which we had recently acquired, and began to speak of the deep meanings hidden within the verses. We urged him to keep the copy. This edition was printed with a single stanza placed at the top of each page, leaving the remainder entirely blank. Swami began to write beneath each verse. His full rendition of the inner significance of the entire poem appeared in succeeding issues of the *SRF Magazine*. He told me afterward, "It was all that unused space on every page that encouraged me to write the spiritual interpretations." He said it with a twinkle in his eyes, admitting his very natural reaction to those spaces.

My Guru saw my chess set one day, and remarked, "One has so little time to realize God completely." He did not suggest that one withdraw from wholesome recreations, but I saw the truth he was imparting to me. It pertains to the number of things we allow to absorb priceless hours. We can choose what is of value to us. It was an important remark in my life because it led me to note which activities fill the hours (apart from duties) and to be aware of what interests absorb one's thoughts. I found many activities can be enjoyed, on occasion, without need for endless repetition.

Mother once asked Master what he did when women came to him for consultation and were flirtatiously inclined. Master said with a chuckle, "I discuss transcendentalism with them. That discourages them completely."

We had a little copper container with water from the Ganges River sealed in it. Mother gave it to Swami and it seemed to please him. Many years later, when I had been away from Mt. Washington for a while, and returned to see my Guru, he greeted me and then placed this memento in my hand, asking if I remembered it. It was such a thoughtful gesture. This object, forgotten until that instant, brought back these days at Santa Barbara that Mother and I had been privileged to share with him.

Swami was turning the pages of a photograph album one afternoon, seeing each picture with apparent interest but without any comment until he came to one of a three-year-old child (myself) standing on a chair, possessing a serious expression. He pointed to it and said, "The Little Lecturer." His remark was an accurate forecast of the years when I later lectured and gave SRF classes.

Master concluded these Santa Barbara classes with the special *Kriya Initiation.* I wrote in my diary, "I treasure this Initiation—gift of God through the blessings of the Gurus. These teachings are the most wonderful to bring the joy of God-contact."

This was the first of many times I was to receive Kriya from my Guru. The beautiful ceremony that accompanies Kriya helps to impress its holy purpose in the consciousness of the devotee.

Swami often talked and meditated with us by the fireplace. One evening he asked me to "think about lecturing for Yogoda." He knew my interest was to serve in his work but I had not thought of lecturing until then. After his classes were completed he returned to Los Angeles. I received this letter from him soon afterward.

Kamala, 1933

February 8, 1933

Dear Kamala,

I am so glad to receive your letter and to know your Mother's greetings. I am enclosing a lecture schedule for Hollywood for your friends. It is wonderful to see you cooperate with Yogoda. *That is what I wanted always for you to do.* I will give you a copy of all my lectures and back numbers of the *East-West (SRF) Magazine* for preparation in lecturing. I wonder if you would come on the 26th to talk things over. It is necessary to have thorough planning.

With unceasing blessings to you and your Mother,

Swami Yogananda

I went to Mt. Washington on the date he mentioned. Mother was working on a translation and remained in Santa Barbara for the present. I attended Swami's advanced classes given in Hollywood, which included a Kriya ceremony. A Los Angeles lecture series followed and I remained to help with the book-selling, and in other ways where needed. When his manager was called away unexpectedly, I also served in that capacity.

It was a busy, active life. Master was granting half-hour interviews during the daytime, so we were in town by 8 a.m., and his consultations continued without pause until late each day, then back to Mt. Washington for perhaps an hour until evening classes.

Before leaving for his lecture, Master would cross his living room and stand in reverent silence before a large picture of his Guru, Sri Yukteswar. How treasured the Guru is, within the heart of the disciple—this tie based on an eternal bond that does not change.

When the evening talk and interviews were over we returned home to have the late-waiting dinner which Master shared with two other disciples and myself. There was a time for quiet, or a few duties, then meditation and usually to bed by 4 a.m. Instant sleep! This period of sleeping just three hours nightly without any naps lasted exactly one month and when Mother came to Los Angeles we were astonished to see that I had gained ten needed pounds during this short time. It seemed miraculous. However, disciples close to Master are able to testify to similar blessings.

My Preceptor sometimes asked me to type certain of his talks from my notes. I recall once continuing on through the night in order to complete them by morning. Everyone retired to sleep or to meditate, while my typewriter continued on through the hours. As I transcribed the last page, early that spring morning, it was growing light. Later in the day Master asked, "Did you finish it?" I presented it to him and his approving comment was upon my self-chosen perseverance rather than for the manuscript. I felt no tiredness; energy and well-being were always noted when one was serving our Guru.

Swami has written that before he met Sri Yukteswar he had imbibed the erroneous idea that a devotee need not concern himself over-strenuously with worldly duties but that under his training he "soon recovered from the agreeable delusions of irresponsibility." His Guru admired practical people and said, "Divine perceptions are not incapacitating!"

On one memorable day Sri Yukteswar bestowed upon Swami the experience of Cosmic Consciousness, with a touch.* While my Guru was still immersed in that Infinite Bliss, Sri Yukteswar then very calmly and unpretentiously handed him a broom and said, "Come, let us sweep the balcony floor; then we shall walk by the Ganges." Master realized his Guru was teaching him the secret of *balanced living.* While the body performs its daily duties the soul should remain absorbed in Cosmic Beatitude.

Master's teachings and guidance emphasized balanced living: life actively serviceful with duties conscientiously performed, yet always with time for God. He once said to me, "Meditation alone makes one impractical and dreamy— way up in the clouds. The way to real salvation is a combination of both meditation and practical activity."

*Described in *Autobiography of a Yogi.*

83

CHAPTER 8

My Guru Ordains Me a Minister

WHEN summer arrived I went to Colorado to remain for a time at our mountain cabin. While there, I transcribed some of Swami's recent class talks. These typed lessons, sent to Mt. Washington, were later included in the Praecepta Course of Studies. I was also preparing for Yogoda (SRF) lectures and classes which I would be giving later.

Swami was in Seattle, Washington, for another series of talks, and I received a letter from him soon after his arrival there.

June 15, 1933

Dear Kamala,

Though I could not write to you earlier as you know I have been in thickest battle of activities and constant moving—yet *I have daily blessed you*. You left with us a trail of your fragrant divine behavior and efficient help. We have all very much missed you. Your telegram and letters were deeply appreciated.

SAMUEL J. WHITMORE, CHAIRMAN OF BOARD
BARNEY L. ALLIS, PRESIDENT & GEN'L. MGR.

Hotel Muehlebach

BALTIMORE AVENUE
AND TWELFTH STREET

Kansas City, Mo.

To Morrisson Hotel
Chicago Ill.

Dear Kamala,

Could not write
for lack of time
But spiritually bless
you every day
Stopping at Kansas
on way to Chicago,
Cable you come on
Sep 10th 8 P.M. When
I lecture at Morrisson
in World's greatest Parliament
of Religions in "World Unity"
Representatives of 200 religions
joining.

Master Writes That He Will Speak at the Congress of Religions
at the Chicago World's Fair in 1933

I had two weeks campaign in Tacoma. It rained heavily just before I went there and rained in torrents after I left but not during the talks. I had almost 800 people attend—very responsive. I have come to serve all with God.

Meditate each night and day. I meditated 7 days in Elsinore (So. California). It was indescribably perfect. So wish that you had been there. Will be here in Seattle one month. Write to me.

With deepest blessings,

Swami Yogananda

Master's name was on the roster of speakers at the World's Congress of Religions, which was held at the Chicago World's Fair that fall. He wrote from Kansas City to ask if I could attend.

Dear Kamala,

Could not write for lack of time but spiritually bless you every day. Stopping at Kansas on way to Chicago. Can't you come on September 10th, 8 p.m. when I lecture at the Morrison Hotel in World's greatest Parliament of Religions on "World Unity"? Representatives of 200 religions joining.

Boundless blessings always, SY

It was especially fitting that Swami Yogananda would be a representative at a Congress of Religious Unity, for he always emphasized the unity underlying all religions through perception of the One Omnipresent Spirit.

Barriers dissolve without need for outer conformity when there is a spiritual bond. My Guru taught that the diverse religions are branches of *God's one tree of Truth.* He reminded us that Omnipresent Spirit "cannot be walled in by man-made, man-interpreted, man-prescribed beliefs and limitations." The "chorus of many-voiced religions" unite at the altar of our One Father, God.

His great and universal inclusion of all, within his heart and teachings, is expressed in his book *Whispers from Eternity,* which he "Dedicated unto

All the soul-temples of Christians, Moslems, Buddhists,
    Hebrews and Hindus,
Wherein the Cosmic Heart is throbbing equally always—
        And unto
All the multi-colored lamps of various true teachings,
In which shines the same one white flame of God—
        And unto
All churches, mosques, viharas, tabernacles, and temples of
    the world—
Wherein our own One Father dwells impartially in the
    fullness of His glory."

I traveled to Chicago from Colorado, and heard his talk, "Realizing World Unity through the Art of Living." There were several disciples present from Mt. Washington, as well as the many devoted students who had come from various parts of America to hear him speak.

As I listened to Master in the large auditorium at the Morrison Hotel, I again beheld an aura of Light surrounding him. All through the years whenever I saw his aura, it was a Pure Brightness of Light. A Blue radiance extended beyond this Light and haloed his head; a Golden glow outlined the Light around his body.

Following his address I was present at a brief gathering of SRF members. A picture was taken of Master with everyone grouped around him. It was often his way to indicate where he wished each to be, and he would thoughtfully yet quickly arrange the seating.

The next day I joined the group going with him to view the vast Fair grounds and the displays of progress. He was keenly interested in all realms of endeavor, and observed man's achievements with understanding and appreciation.

Master asked me to see him on the following morning. I had the blessing of a visit with him, and then returned to Colorado.

I was staying in the heart of the Rocky Mountains. This was always my happiest childhood environment, with its cinerama of gigantic rocks, streams, wild-flowers, golden sunrises, and winds singing through the trees. In summer every shade of green spells peace to the soul; then autumn turns the hillsides into a Persian carpet of rich tones. Winter snows soon come, casting a spell of silence everywhere, while the bright sun spreads a sparkle of diamonds across this scene of enchantment. O God Beautiful, so visible!

It was here, many years later, that this book was commenced with the re-reading of my Guru's letters. An inner intuition guided my thoughts to the realization that it was Master's wish, and for a time I daydreamed over memories. Then I began to type, and the first page started to unfold these recollections wherein I would share the letters, poems, and conversations of this man of God.

At this present time I was writing some articles that were currently appearing in the *SRF Magazine*. These included a three-part series on the life of Buddha entitled "The Life of Prince Siddhartha." It was a condensation of Edwin Arnold's poetic *Light of Asia*.

One writing touched upon the subject of reincarnation. Whether one accepts the theory of reincarnation or not, there are many things in life which cause us to stop and ponder. If we do not accept this, there seem to be many effects without any apparent causes. Reincarnation gives meaning to the seeming inconsistencies in life. Cause and effect can then be viewed extending beyond one short lifespan.

*I was ordained a minister of the Self-Realization Fellowship
by Paramhansa Yogananda in 1934.*

Our desires and karma propel the soul into the environment needed and earned. Often it is a reversal of the many
other roles we have known. Swami said that God gives us
"fresh chances to be better in a new unrecognizable body
and in another environment."

We seldom recall the distant past of other lives. Forgetful-
ness is an undoubted blessing! We would hardly be capable
of sufficient detachment if we remembered all of the sad and
happy experiences, and recognized all relationships of the
past. The old attitudes, fears and tensions, loves, attachments,
and prejudices would color the new life. Yet nothing is lost.
Our total capabilities—mental, physical, and spiritual—remain inherent, and reappear expressly as tendencies,
inclinations, and gifted abilities.

My Guru taught about reincarnation, yet he did not consider belief in it to be a necessary prerequisite in the devotee's
search for God. With the infallible perception and vision of a
Master, he could look into his own past lives and those of
others, but he did not dwell upon our changing roles. He
turned our attention to the Indwelling Self and to our own
eternal identity with God. He once said to me, "Concentrate
on the immortality, not on the changes."

When Christmas time was near, I sent a gift that I hoped
might please my Guru. The selection was a small watch with
a jeweled Swiss movement. It gave a view of the mechanism
through the crystal cover. His letter from California speaks of
the watch.

January 5, 1934

Dear Kamala,

I am overwhelmed and deeply touched to have you send me the gift. I am playing with it like a child with a new toy. After a long time I have found something in the material world to interest me. I am carrying it in my vest and using it with a watch chain.

Do write me often. I am never so busy that I do not have time for the pleasure of reading your letters.

Many many times I send you a thousand blessings through God.

Meditate deeply and do Kriya.

Swami Yogananda

I was receiving these blessings, for this was a time of many inner realizations. Another letter from Master reached me shortly.

January 25, 1934

Dear Kamala,

How are you getting along? When are you planning to set out on *your spiritual mission of spreading Self-Realization Fellowship?* Please let me know.

Fond wishes from all of the Sisters.

With deepest blessings from me.

Swami Yogananda

I returned to California and was often with my Guru at
Mt. Washington as he made plans for a trip to India. It was
at this time that *Master ordained* me a minister of the Self-
Realization Fellowship. This was without formal ceremony
but with special blessing.

Before his journey he said to me, "When I return I am
going to live at Mt. Washington all the time. Do you want to
come here to live permanently?" I expressed an eagerness to
impart his teachings to others in many areas, and this caused
me to make a decision for service on the outside. My Guru
was instantly ready to help me in my plans. Soon afterward
Master gave a Kriya Initiation in the Chapel. He told me, "I
want you to sit in front and watch the ceremony very carefully so you will be able to give Kriya. Take notes on everything
in detail."

(I went to Arizona shortly afterward, where I gave a series
of lectures and classes; then I continued to give instruction in
SRF Lessons in Colorado and California.)

One day near his sailing date we had been talking in
Master's living room, and our conversation continued as we
stood in the hall by his doorway. It was then that I remarked
that if he wished me to teach all of the lessons, I had not

received a certain advanced Initiation. He said instantly, "Oh, it is this way." Then, without ceremony and with complete simplicity, he gave the techniques of the 3rd and 4th Initiations to me. They have helped me tremendously in my deeper meditations.

CHAPTER 9

Blessings of Grace

INNER realizations have come from God through my Guru's blessing. They are treasures which I have received with wonder, and have filled my being. In each instance there is upliftment, ranging from deep peace to a great joy, and at times the bliss of God. Accompanying each is always a profound inner tranquility. These wonderful states of upliftment fill one *during* the experience and *continue for some time afterward*. They bring an inexpressible glow to heart and soul.

As we open the door to God, through love and devotion, there comes Expansion of Consciousness in which we know moments—even hours—of the Peace-Joy-Bliss states. Such soul communion surpasses all outward manifestation which may accompany it. Happenings that are only extra-sensory, however spectacular or amazing they may be, are savorless without *God's tremendous blessedness*. God is the Salt! He is the Sugar!

The sacred blessings I have received never have been revealed—even to those near and dear. I would have known immeasurable loss to have spoken of them. It is only now, with an inner Divine sanction, that I am including several of them here, as written in my diary notes beginning in 1925.

Emerson said that soul manifestations are revelations in which the individual soul mingles with the Universal Soul; that such times are always attended with feelings of the sublime. The instances presented here give some of the diverse ways that the varied intensities of spiritual feeling have come to me.

Golden Rain

After this evening lecture by Swami, I returned home, and as I walked in the door, before turning on the light, the rooms were *raining golden light.* It was golden rain everywhere, from ceiling to floor. The raindrops were very long and golden in the darkened house. It kept raining gold after the lights were on. I turned them off, again on, but it was the same. Then, I left them off for about ten minutes while I sat looking with wide-open eyes! Shortly there was the sound of a car coming round the hill, and it all ceased instantly. A *serene* feeling was with me during this unusual vision—a *peacefulness* that seemed part of it.

In his *Autobiography* Master has written of "pencilled rays, like sheets of rain" and these words describe that scene. I recall thinking, as I sat there, that my Guru had opened my eyes to this vision of subtle rays, and was aware of my seeing them.

Samadhi

In sleep, I was standing beside a precipice. Completely aware, I said, "I know that I am dreaming and this a dream body. I am soul, one with Spirit; so I will go over." Then I dived—to prove fearlessness. Instantly, at the moment I would have touched the earth below, there came a *whirling light in the forehead* and the *encompassing rush of sound.* I was drawn into this light as in a Whirlpool, and at the same time the Om assumed thunderous proportions and sounded everywhere at once. Then both Light and Sound ceased, *merging into Bliss*—perfect beyond all description.

This immersion into the Bliss of God was the most complete I had known, for there ceased to be any "I" when this came. All was *Bliss* and I had become a part of it! I was awake in consciousness but the material world was forgotten. An afterglow of the blissfulness lingered long after I met the day and its activities.

Floating Tour

I awoke seeing my Guru standing before me. Suddenly my breath stopped for a long time, and I sailed over vast continents and oceans; floated over mountain parks of evergreen, and hillsides of snow-covered trees. I felt the *joy* of being in such beauty everywhere! This came with a sentience beyond ordinary intensity, and I absorbed, with detailed clarity, all that I saw upon the beautiful earth.

X-ray Vision

Growing conscious during sleep, I saw outside of the house and way down the street. At the same time I could see the interior of this room and view my body asleep. I saw the street as it was at that moment in the early morning—not a remembered view of it, or a dream view. My place of vantage was above the sleeping body, seeing down upon it as well as viewing the walls, and also through them, beyond—much as an x-ray can do. Everything was so clear, and I was completely awake within some center of quietness. It was all very still during this amazing sojourn into a new dimension of vision.

Conscious sleep, mentioned here and in some other instances in this chapter, is a state of awareness while the body continues sleeping. It is much like deep meditation, in which the body and outer sensations are temporarily forgotten. Instead of the unconsciousness of sleep, there is the same cognizance as when awake.

God's Healing Answer

I was thinking of a problem and went into every aspect of it, seeking God's help. Then suddenly I felt soothing Peace like healing balm, and *Joy flooding my heart*. I said aloud to God: "When You give the Grace of Your Presence, this is all one wants!" All concern over the problem had ceased. My heart was alight in *God's glowing presence.* It was a flow of super-Joy that lasted many hours—about 36.

Precious Awakening

This morning God wakened me so sweetly, so gently, like silently-falling snow. Very hard to describe. I was aware of the *vibrating ethers* everywhere in the room.

Taste Delight

At meditation I experienced a taste subtle beyond any earth-known delicacy. It was present without the thought of swallowing. I have known Divine inner sound, inner sight, and fragrances, but never before have known inner taste.

Ascent through Vibrations

Quietly resting with closed eyes, I was drawn inward and *up,* through *every degree* of Consciousness to a Peace beyond all describing. I passed from the solidity of flesh and weight, beyond gravitational laws to where there were no restricting boundaries, no weight, just a wonderful awareness of *Eternity,* peace-filled. Then in exact reverse, coming down through all degrees and being part of each one, sensitively a part, this normal weight was like heavy metal after being lighter than air. Opening my eyes, I was "here," closing them, I was "there." I longed to remain in that heavenly freedom where one is so light.

Then I realized how much a sense of lightness or heaviness depends upon our state of consciousness. This seems to be the manner in which God separates the different planes—through gradations of gross and fine vibrations. Sense of body weight, and material consciousness in ourselves, creates its own barriers. I experienced this one night, in another way, a little time after my Father had passed on.

Doorway to Light

My Father came to me when I was asleep. I could see he wanted me to accompany him and that he felt a sense of urgency, as if he knew he could not linger. He led me to a large Church which we entered, and we went up a stairway. When we reached the landing-platform we had a view of the immense place of worship beneath: great spaciousness, rich woods, and carpeted floors, with the simplicity of many Protestant churches. Beyond this was a second flight of stairs—a very wide staircase of about a dozen steps. Standing a moment on this landing, I looked up and at the top there was an open Doorway. Through it was *mystic Light* like Illumined Mist. So beautiful! The Mystery of Silence pervaded that Doorway. We both started up but I could walk only three or four steps before I became conscious of weight and stood there unable to go any further. My Father was evidently ready for this advanced state, for he went up lightly, and then on through the Doorway *into* that *Light*.

Thought Communication

At the beach cottage this afternoon I felt an unusual sense of relaxation, and almost at once my Guru, who was at Mt. Washington, spoke through my mind, telling me that he was coming to the beach, and named those whom he was bringing with him. He conveyed this through his positive will, showing me "thought communication." I received it in my relaxed state of receptivity. He arrived later today and with him was each one he had named.

Contrasting Forces

Had an interesting happening in conscious sleep. I traveled down a long sunny road with high trees on both sides. Suddenly all of my being was tossed into dark space— terrifically tossed—as one would shake corn in a popper! I felt I had been entirely lifted by some force and thrown, and I could do nothing about it. I was not frightened and said, "It doesn't matter what happens, God, for Thou Art with me here, the same as anywhere"—and then I was gently, oh so gently, out of the darkness and again in the bed. From the gentle way I was returned I believe it was some kind of a test.

Spiritual Currents

It was after meditation with Swami, about half an hour later when going to my room, that *waves* of *currents* passed from head to foot, so that I could hardly walk. They had great force. I was uplifted and sensed God's Presence around me.

Kriya Blessing

At one of Swami's lectures this week I knew a great downpouring of spiritual blessings while I was taking lecture notes in shorthand. I had the sensation of electricity in the spine. Swami said right afterward, "I have never seen you so happy."

Many Waters

The *Om* came in a great *rushing Sound* like a waterfall.* I was so still—in deepest Contentment.

Celestial Music

During sleep heard beautiful *Music* like a symphony filling the skies with its sounds—then awoke still hearing it, and Waves of Divine Vibrations went through me, over and over, giving a Christ-like Peace that was a part of this harmony.

Rapture

Awoke *seeing the Light,* and felt *exultation* for hours. This feeling accompanied the Light.

---

*Bible: ". . . his voice as the sound of many waters."
—Revelation 1:15
"His voice was like a noise of many waters: and the earth shined with his glory."
—Ezekiel 43:2

Cosmic Bliss

I grew conscious, during sleep, and saw Swami walking toward me. I realized he was *in samadhi* so I touched him, and I was *instantly immersed in Cosmic Bliss* by his direct blessing. This Bliss continued on through this day, even in all of my activities—untouched by anything. I felt God as Supreme *Happiness*—indescribable.

These inner realizations appear as they were recorded long ago. It was my habit to condense rather than to write fully. Their brevity may not impart the overwhelming impact of the Divine manifestations but I hope will suggest it.

Direct insight into spheres of soul-perception brings personal verification of our being an integral part of Eternity. Our own (indestructible) Consciousness can merge with Omnipresent Spirit, and instead of individual awareness dissolving or diminishing, it increases.

The words of the ancient sage, Kabir, have special meaning when one perceives that he described not symbolic ideas but actual soul experiences. I quote from his song-poem translated by Rabindranath Tagore.

It is the mercy of my true Guru that

Has made me know the unknown;

I have learned from him how to walk

Without feet, to see without eyes,
To hear without ears, to drink
Without mouth, to fly without wings.
Without eating, I have tasted of the
Sweetness of nectar; and without
Water, I have quenched my thirst.
Kabir says: "The Guru is great beyond words
and great is the good fortune of the disciple."

CHAPTER 10

Early Recollections

MANY children express a deep interest in God. I can remember several times in childhood trying to picture *what was* before the beginning of time; in the vastness before anything existed, how God was there! Mother once reminisced about the time I was small and came to her with the question, "Who made God?" She replied that she did not know. I went away but returned after some time to inform her matter-of-factly: "I know who made God." She smiled and asked, "You do?" "Yes, He made Himself," was my self-found answer! The wonder of Life and its Mystery is implanted in our souls. Is it our Creator softly calling to us?

If I turn my thoughts back to childhood, my first memory in this life is at the age of three—an experience of seeming significance. I can recall it as vividly as at that hour.

I was lying ill with scarlet fever, with an unduly high temperature. The nurse in the room told Mother later that I had spent the time lying in the bed unmoving, and with eyes half-open and unblinking. In consciousness, however, I had not been there. I had been on a journey.

The wall at the head of my bed had opened into a tunnel, and slowly the bed began to move into it and on through this dark route, as if on railway tracks. The movement was slow and steady and the very slowness seemed to preserve a sense of quietness. The bed was seemingly directed by some unseen force.

After a short time I emerged into daylight, where I could see a river. There were trees near its low banks and sheep were contentedly feeding. The shepherd, Christ-like in appearance, stood with peaceful serenity. He was turned toward me, but I could not tell if he saw me. Reluctant as I was to leave this scene, the conveying bed did not pause but continued on across the bridge which spanned the river.

Then the way led again into a tunnel on the farther bank and we went on into pitch darkness as before, with the walls so narrow I could have touched them if I had put my arms out beyond the bedsides.

After a short distance, we came to a solid blocking in the passageway and the bed jarred unexpectedly to a stop. Here "we" (the bed and I) were motionless. I sensed this barrier was not anticipated and that our goal was beyond. We were waiting for a door or wall to open! We remained waiting there for some minutes in the inky darkness. There was complete stillness.

Then—very, very slowly the bed moved in reverse direction on a return journey. Soon it was going at its former pace, except this time I was facing the way we were moving as I lay there. We emerged again into the daylight, with the open countryside and the river once more visible. We crossed the bridge to reach the scene I was awaiting! I beheld its beauty and saw the shepherd as before, but we were soon re-entering the dark tunnel, which led back into my own room. Once there, the bed came to a halt with a slight jar and the wall-opening closed. I was back!

I called to my Mother instantly, related my journey, and told her, "I want to go back to the beautiful place, but I want you to sit on the bed and hold my hand while we go through the dark part."

With natural concern Mother questioned the nurse who was sitting there. But there was no need, for this was the turning place in my long illness and soon I was well.

It was at the age of 16 that another unusual experience came to me. One afternoon I had been reading from Emerson's *Essays,* and afterward fell asleep for a brief nap. I awakened hearing a *choir* of *thousands* of voices in exquisite harmony. My diary described it, "like an Angels' Choir." I had been hearing it in sleep but it kept on long after I awakened, and I remained still, listening to it. I was lifted into pure Joyousness.

I recall so vividly the impact of this stirringly beautiful music on my heart and mind, and the sense of Buoyancy amounting to a Bliss state that followed. I have since realized that its length of duration of a week was an added rare blessing.

Childhood Picture Master
Called "The Little Lecturer"

CHAPTER 11

The Autobiography of a Yogi

MASTER remained abroad for one and a half eventful years. His travels included visits to the Holy Land, Europe, England, Scotland, and many parts of India. He lectured to immense gatherings in India, and also in England, sponsored by leading citizens in both countries.

In London the press and newsreel photographers recorded his activities. A newspaper columnist wrote in the *London Star:* "I managed to squeeze into Caxton Hall before the overflow invaded the Press table. The occasion was an address on 'God' by Swami Yogananda, Yoga master. Hall, floor and balconies were crammed. For an hour-and-a-quarter attention was held. I have heard few equals of the Swami as an orator. There was not a syllable of rant or unintelligible metaphysic. At the end of 75 minutes the Swami, apparently not the least fatigued, left to address the overflow meetings."

India also accorded him a magnificent welcome, honoring his return after 15 years. While he was there his Guru, Sri Yukteswar, bestowed upon him the title of *Paramhansa*, which

Sri Yukteswar of the Giri (Mountain) Branch of the Swami Order of Renunciates Founded by Swami Shankaracharya Many Centuries Ago in India

means "Supreme Swan" (symbolically, a vehicle of the Infinite). It fitted well my Preceptor, whose life had been lived to carry disciples to the shores of God-Realization.

After Master's return to California he spent much time continuing the writing of his *Autobiography*. When completed, he gave me a copy of the book. His priceless gift was followed by this letter.

March 17, 1947

Dear Kamala,

Thank you for your very kind words about my autobiography. I deeply appreciate them. It makes me very happy to know that the work to which I devoted 25 years in the writing is being so well received everywhere. That is due to God's Blessing, for I prayed this book would strengthen the desire of every reader to seek Him with great determination and zeal.

Your letter of appreciation made me happy—now spread our message of Self-Realization through the book—as you have always been a champion of our cause.

With blessings,
Paramhansa Yogananda

Paramhansa Yogananda has enabled one to become acquainted with him and with each of the *Paramgurus* through the pages of his book. His *Autobiography of a Yogi* reaches out to the questing seeker with wisdom, love, and endearing humor. Young readers and lifetime students are equally enriched by the contents, which inspire one to drink deeply at the well of Spirit.

The magnitude of this treasured classic in Divine Pilgrimage cannot be appreciated fully with one or two readings. Comprehension of its worth is a growing experience. It encompasses aspects of wisdom that are newly revealed upon each viewing.

He gives a detailed history of the way the teachings were brought to us through the Paramgurus. Anciently taught by *Krishna,* it was *Babaji,* Himalayan Avatar, who initiated *Lahiri Mahasaya* into Kriya Yoga. This revered disciple, who was a householder, achieved supreme Realization. Babaji assured him that "the millions who have family ties and are encumbered by heavy worldly duties will take new heart from you, a householder like themselves." It was Lahiri Mahasaya's advanced disciple, *Sri Yukteswar,* who became the Preceptor of *Yogananda.**

In his childhood and early youth Yogananda had a great desire to know God. He felt that to do so he must find his own Guru. His account of the long search for this man of God (Sri Yukteswar) allows us to travel with him on his quest. He recounts many interesting and unusual meetings

*This chosen monastic name, "Yogananda," means "divine bliss through union (yoga) with the Infinite."

with men and women of holy reputation. His immense longing for Cosmic Consciousness was fulfilled through the
enlightened guidance of his Guru. He describes this tremendous experience in his book.

Sri Yukteswar, a renunciate of the Swami Order, was highly
regarded in his country, and by all who knew him. He believed the approach to God should be scientific, and he was
widely known for his expositions on the Bible and Bhagavad-
Gita. He elucidated their deep meanings in his book *The
Holy Science*, wherein he has shown the basic unity within the
scriptures of the two books.

Master's trip in 1935 was planned when Sri Yukteswar
asked him to return to India at that special time. This great
Rishi knew of his coming transition. He passed on while
Master was there. Sri Yukteswar's after-death return to his
loved disciple, Paramhansa Yogananda, took place in a scene
that gives mankind great insight into the "many mansions"
of heaven. This is recounted in one of the chapters of his
Autobiography of a Yogi.

This book has been translated into many languages, and
also into braille. It carries the message of Kriya Yoga, which
is known as the great "spiritual accelerator."

Paramhansa Yogananda is responsible for the advent of
Kriya Yoga in the Western world. He has written, "Kriya,
controlling the mind directly through the life force, is the

easiest, most effective, and most scientific avenue of approach to the Infinite." This teaching is in accord with his life's purpose, which he described in these lines:

> I come to tell you all of Him, and the way to encase Him in your bosom, and of the discipline that brings His Grace, to those of you who have asked me to guide you to my Beloved's Presence.

Master was welcomed home from his travels by the residents and guests at Mt. Washington, Christmas 1936. Master in foreground with Rajarsi, a disciple. I appear at left. Paramhansa recounted this happy occasion in chapter 47 of his Autobiography.

CHAPTER 12

Life at Mt. Washington

A few years had passed with Master's guidance and blessing always present. I was soon to be living at Mt.
Washington and a double rainbow seemed to preface this
new move in my life.

I was taking a trip by bus and in the early morning, after a
light rain, *two rainbows* appeared. One of them dipped to the
right of the bus; the other one dropped into the road a little
distance ahead of us. We rode for miles with both staying in
the same positions in relation to the bus. The colors were
amazingly close by! The rainbows accompanied me almost to
my destination and I felt a breath-taking sense of wonder.
From the moment they had appeared, I knew an intense
awareness of *Master's Presence* as well as of each of our
Paramgurus. It made the hour unforgettable and one filled
with spiritual promise.

An elderly woman was sitting beside me. She had the
appearance of culture and refinement. She had not spoken to
me previously; just a friendly nod when we first sat down.
But now she said, "I often take this trip but I never have seen
this before. I believe it means something good for you."

Surely the "pot of gold" of a rainbow is to be found most truly at the feet of one's Guru, so it seemed a confirmation of her words when upon my return to Los Angeles Master telephoned me. He wished for me to see him after church on Sunday. On that day he asked me if I could come immediately to Mt. Washington to serve. I was then working in the offices of the Community Chest. I answered that I would make arrangements, but inquired if he wished me to come, since I did not plan to become a renunciate. He answered that this was accepted since it was understood between us. We talked in serious vein, and in conclusion he said, "I will send a car for you."

The morning I arrived at Mt. Washington, Master met and welcomed me and expressed happiness that I was there. The disciples greeted me with love.

Paramhansaji wished me to serve in the Letter-Writing Department and I remained in this special work for the next fifteen months.

The day's activities began when a soft gong bell announced the hour for the women to assemble on the front porch for morning exercise, which consisted of the SRF re-energizing exercises. This was followed by a period of worship in the Chapel. After breakfast the regular office hours began. The Praecepta lessons, books, magazine, and all of the literature were mailed from here. The vast world-wide correspondence was also carried on, shared by the Monks in their separate

Snow Scene at Mt. Washington. Unusual snowfall presents lovely view of the Self-Realization Fellowship premises.

working quarters. The men disciples operated the printing press. The cooking, gardening, and general housekeeping was in the care of those not occupied with office work, and rarely did the work of one department overlap into that of another. Each disciple kept his own room in order.

While working in the office there were occasions when Master called me on the house interphone. He would converse in his gracious way that was without any sense of hurry. There were comfortable silences, just as when with him. I felt very close to him and a sense of deep peace followed the talks.

It was natural that anyone who did not work with Master directly saw him less frequently, which was true of that period when I served there. However, many recollections of those days come to mind.

I was going down the stairs one day when I heard my Guru call someone. His voice was resonant with a vibrant golden tone. I stood still, thinking how his spoken word reflected spiritual beauty through sound. It stirred me deeply and remembrance of it remains with me.

When it was known that Master was going out in the car, everyone liked to go to the entrance near the stairway where he would come down. These were cherished moments, for he would greet each one who was standing in the large foyer, and silently bless with a touch of his hand on one's forehead, perhaps a few words. When he walked through the doorway to step into the waiting car everyone followed to the front porch. His sweet smile encompassed all, until the car moved down the driveway from view.

Whenever my Guru spoke of my Mother it was with warm regard. The last few months of her life had been ones of enforced inactivity due to a severe heart condition. It had been my happy privilege to care for her. She made a beautiful afghan for me during this time. It has served ever since in my morning meditations, placed about my shoulders. It is not possible to say easily or briefly the depth of my feeling for her. Her passing was naturally a great loss to me. She had always given me love and companionship and comforted me with her lifelong caring. Is one ever prepared for this parting? Myriad tender remembrances of her are etched in mind and heart. She left me with a memory of her love.

Once when Master mentioned my Mother to a group of disciples, he described her as "a wonderful Mother, so understanding." One day when talking with Master, he noticed an unusual necklace I was wearing, and he spoke of it. I told him that it had been my Mother's, and he said, "Oh" in a tone of loving sweetness. He put his hands on the stones, gently touching them, as if a blessing in her memory.

Responsiveness was a part of my Guru; it came from his heart, immediate and sincere, with a warmth you could feel. I never found him aloof or indifferent.

One afternoon a friend of mine came to seek Paramhansa's advice as to what to do with her life. He included this suggestion in his talk with her: "Since the past cannot be changed, begin today with where you are." This wisdom cautioned one not to look back with "ifs." Long ago I wrote to his dictation: "The fish that swims away was the biggest fish; the happiness that was not fully enjoyed seems to be the biggest one lost."

An unexpected encounter with Master occurred late one night when I went to the kitchen for matches to light my heater. I expected to see no one at all. Instead, Master was sitting at the table and there were also several members of the household with him. He asked me to remain, and his words of greeting were to tell me that he had been thinking of going on a drive to Manhattan Beach, and of calling me to accompany him, but he had not been able to get away. Then he related an incident to us which took place during his trip to India. Someone who had lost the ability to walk unaided had turned to him for healing. Intuitively, he knew that effort must be made, and a long, difficult walk was taken with Master assisting, encouraging, and praying. Recovery followed. I received a clear impression that his willingness to help, in this instance, implied his acceptance of the karmic problem and the responsibility for it.

Karmic debt is not always assumed by another when healing takes place. Master has explained that it is sometimes done in the way a father may assume the debts of a son, if he wishes. In all instances, Master made one aware of God as the Healer. God's healing is received in various ways. Potent forces include faith, will power, and life energy. Healing therapy is found through repetition of a chosen affirmation. Love, kindness, happiness, forgiveness, and thanksgiving each have healing power. Prayer is a tremendous force for Divine healing. Environment and karma are important factors. God's laws are present in all the processes of healing of the body as well as the mind. Foods and medicines are composed of rates of vibrations which correspond to specific needs. To benefit one, they must be wisely chosen. With his writings, Paramhansaji* has spoken of healings[†] many times, but he sought primarily to awaken love for God, because this remains an eternal blessing. He did not ever measure spiritual attainment by the degree of bodily health, since strong men have not necessarily become masters of wisdom as a result of their physical perfection. But he taught the practice of healthful living, giving it importance. On this night he inquired about the meals, showing a concern over proper nutrition for the disciples, and instructed the kitchen staff to increase the daily

---

*"ji" = A term of respect often added to a name or title: Sri Yukteswarji, Babaji, Yoganandaji.

[†]*Scientific Healing Affirmations* by Paramhansa Yogananda describes many aspects of this subject.

protein foods in the vegetarian diet that provided a wide variety without meat.

Many of the disciples at Mt. Washington are renunciates of the SRF Order of Sisters but there are also newer student resident workers who come to serve and evaluate a decision for this way of life. These novices are placed wherever their abilities lie, yet they must be equally willing to fit in anywhere they are needed. This applies to both Sisters and Monks.

Divine inner experiences are held sacred. I have never heard the telling of them among the women disciples. The closest happening in this regard took place at a meal many years before, when a renunciate Sister began to tell of a vision she had received through Master's blessing. She was describing, very simply, an account of the unusual incident. Our Guru was sitting beside us but he was occupied with his own thoughts. When Master finally noted the trend of her remarks, he interrupted her narration at once, clearly indicating that he did not wish her to speak of it.

Once, in the past, a disciple did not come to the table; a mood kept her in her room. Master disapproved of moody behavior. He commented briefly upon it, then said no more. His way to teach was with very little verbal reprimand, allowing the disciple to perceive and correct the fault.

Master emphasized "right behavior." He expected our actions to be in keeping with discipline and good conduct, regardless of the way one might feel or think. A right attitude is to be desired, but one may need time to perfect attitudes and tendencies, so when action is required, our Guru taught us to "behave rightly." Thoughts and feelings often surprisingly follow the pattern of the action.

A resident disciple is rarely disturbed in her room by a knock at the door, and any message is put on the floor just outside the room where it will be seen. I have had many notes left with expressions of kindness thoughtfully sent in them, yet not once a sound to disturb meditation, duties, or relaxation.

When I later went to northern California, my Guru counseled: "Do not discuss your personal life with others." This is a rule also observed by disciples at Mt. Washington who follow Master's training. I observed that they did not ask personal questions. In this way tendency to gossip is eliminated. All discussion about personality traits, comments upon the actions, habits, or activities of others, and of one's self, all that makes up usual small talk, is replaced with quietness.

Some of the women renunciates practice the asanas of Hatha Yoga and become proficient in them. Occasionally, at Convocation the men resident disciples demonstrate their skill in these Yoga postures. They are not a part of Master's Praecepta studies, but detailed instructions for the various asanas appear in the *SRF Magazine*. SRF teachings incorporate some of each of the systems of Yoga but emphasize Raja Yoga.

Festive Winter Garb at Mt. Washington from Rare Occurrence of Snow in January 1949

Christmas Day, 1948, Myself on Lawn at the Self-Realization Fellowship Headquarters

For the great majority of people who are not inclined to asana practice it should be noted that in giving yoga instruction, Paramhansaji always taught the posture for meditation is to sit on a chair with spine straight, chin parallel to the ground, the shoulders straight, and hands resting relaxed in one's lap. The lotus posture may be assumed for meditation if it is comfortable and individually preferred, but it is not required.

One day the disciples from the office had gone out to bid goodbye to a departing guest. While we were returning to the front entrance we saw Master sitting at his open window in the morning sunshine. He spoke to some of the disciples who were looking up from the lawn and driveway, and they replied, speaking quietly. I stood very still, looking at him, to be sure of what my eyes beheld. Unlike any experience I had previously known, I saw that Master was *blue-colored*—not an aura but the very texture of his skin was that mystic Christmas blue which is the vibratory color of Christ Consciousness. I went under the portico to think of it. I returned and looked again; then a third time. It was real. I did not want to speak with anyone. I wanted to savor the special vision. Although I was seeing with inner sight, my physical eyes saw it as clearly as one sees that the color of grass is green. I thought afterward of the song "My Krishna is Blue," and that Master had written of Krishna's "divine form of sky-blue rays." It was thus I saw my Guru on this day. It seemed so right, yet amazing to behold with open eyes. I realized that Master was completely at one with Krishna and Christ, and by his grace I was blessed with this vision.

Sermons on Sundays were given regularly by Master at the beautiful SRF Church of All Religions in Hollywood. He instructed with insight and clarity in the precepts needed for daily living, with its many complexities. I was present whenever he talked. He spoke not from notes but from mentally-organized thoughts, given inspirationally, based upon inner realization.

Paramhansaji taught not alone by sermons, but by example. Words come to mind that describe some of the qualities exemplified in his life. *Humbleness* is one, fiber of his being. How beautiful it is to behold this attribute in a person, present under all circumstances! Another is *courtesy*. Through the years I saw its Godly significance in human relationships as it was expressed through all of his words and actions. *Holiness* is another. There was about him a sanctity that radiated from him as veritable as a fragrance. His presence magnetically lifted and drew hearts to God.

One of his prayers, transcribed from my notes, is given here. Paramhansaji said to us: "Close your eyes and feel devotion for our own Father in the Temple of Silence. An aroma of peace fills this Temple. We bring all the flowers of love that grow in the garden of our consciousness. They are decorating our altar of humbleness." Then he prayed:

Come, Spirit, come. Receive the fervor of our souls. We worship Thee with the burning, ringing desire of our hearts; with the chants of our souls. We are Thy children. We are knocking at Thy Door. Receive us!

Spirit Divine, forgive our trespasses; teach us to love our brothers as Thy children. May Thou, the only Spirit, be reflected in the mirror of our souls. Teach us to want Thee, only. It is Thy Love that it is my privilege to spread, with the pollen of reverence. May each one receive Thy Light. Receive our Souls at Thy Feet of Omnipresence.

CHAPTER 13

I Impart My Guru's Teachings

WHEN I left for the Bay Area in northern California Master said, "I am glad you are going there. I will have someone there I can trust. You know my teachings."

When I protested lack of extensive lecture experience, he said, without the slightest regard for my trepidations, "One learns to swim by getting in the water."

I was married during the Christmas holidays, having previously received Master's blessing. I felt a close tie with Edward, from the distant past. Much has corroborated this feeling through the years.

Edward's love for Master's teachings was based upon earlier awareness that religion in India has a universal scope and does not try to circumscribe God into a particular creed, tenet, or church. When I met him I told him about the SRF teachings. He read the *Autobiography of a Yogi* and afterward commented, "I did not want the book ever to end." He became a Praecepta student, and expressed eagerness to hear Paramhansaji speak. His first meeting with Master was at the Hollywood SRF Church. Edward was in the U.S. Navy, then on leave from the South Pacific.

One day Master said to me, "God should always be first." I replied instantly, "Oh, but He is." My reply satisfied him for he told me, "Then it is all right." This referred to my leaving the environment of the Hermitage. Master always held the spiritual progress of the disciple foremost in his thought. His training of each one differed; his guidance was not identical among the renunciates. This was equally true with householder disciples. To write of my own training is not to give a "typical" example, for there were not any two that were just the same.

When we went to Oakland to live, Edward and I visited dozens of addresses to contact members in the Bay Area. We reserved a beautiful room at the Palace Hotel in San Francisco for our weekly meetings that were to begin in the fall, and Master expressed great interest in the establishing of this Center. In April he wrote:

Dear Kamala,

I was extremely delighted to get your greeting—letter of April 11th. I am so happy you and Edward are planning to develop the Center. Please remember my heart and blessings are with you both.

You should have a real Divine hive there with lots of Divine honey in it. Let me know your plans.

Unceasing blessings,
Paramhansa Yogananda

We were away for several weeks during the summer. Upon our return we were soon to have our first SRF meeting. Master speaks of this in his letter.

September 8, 1949

Dear Kamala and Edward,

Am so pleased to have your letter of August 25, and to learn that the opening date of our new Self-Realization Center is set for September 27th. Rest assured that I will be with you in spirit on that day—that this first meeting may be a successful and Divinely inspired one.

I shall be eagerly awaiting a report from you after the meeting has taken place. It brings great joy to my heart, knowing that we have the cooperation of such devoted souls as you and Edward to help disseminate these teachings of God and the Gurus.

Am happy to learn that you enjoyed your trip. Truly, when we are in harmony with the Divine Will, all things run smoothly. You are both being remembered in my daily meditations, that you may steadily progress on the spiritual path.

My love and blessings to you and Edward,

Paramhansa Yogananda

Our SRF plans and activities received from Master his continued spiritual guidance.

September 16, 1949

Dear Kamala and Edward,

I was very happy to receive further news—happy news about starting the Center. May God ever be with you to establish the temple of Self-Realization in the souls of men that He may dwell there to free them.

[Regarding someone in the area] Whenever you can, you both should meditate with him—he needs that. We must teach people to meditate and feel God. *The Church should first teach God-contact* and help create the habit of meditation.

If you follow this theme to meditate yourselves with your close associates in SRF, you will find spiritual members—not followers who are emotionally-drugged on superficially-dipped intellectuality. Bring members to God, Christ and Gurus through their own self-perception of God and the joy of meditation.

With all my love to you both. Give your life to God, Gurus and SRF,

Paramhansa Yogananda

This notice was printed in the *SRF Magazine:*

> The first meeting of a recently organized SRF Center in San Francisco was held September 27th at the Palace Hotel. Those present included residents of San Francisco, Oakland, Berkeley, Hayward, San Leandro, Menlo Park, and even distant San Jose.

Our meetings at the Palace Hotel continued for several years. Later we met in Berkeley, where we held Sunday services. In San Francisco, Oakland, San Jose, and Berkeley I lectured, held classes on the basic techniques, and gave Kriya Initiations twice a year for all members in this area. As a minister I included christenings, marriages, counseling and other ministering offices of a church.

When I attended the 1951 Convocation at Mt. Washington, the printed Calendar of Events included our Center meetings. It stated: "The SRF now has seven Centers in California . . . where you will receive the teachings of Paramhansa Yogananda . . . which have been established to facilitate your search for truth." Listed were three churches (in Hollywood, San Diego, and Long Beach), the Colony at Encinitas, our Center in San Francisco at the Palace Hotel, the new Lake Shrine at Pacific Palisades, and Mt. Washington in Los Angeles.

I always wore a sari for our meetings and asked Paramhansaji on what other occasions I should wear one. He replied, "Whenever you are representing the SRF, and when you are with members, if possible."

Sometimes I consulted our Guru by long-distance calls, regarding our Center work, and these talks would often extend into long and treasured conversations.

Paramhansaji said to me it was good to hold services on Sundays, because that day is associated in the minds of people with church. I found this to be evident in our own groups, for although the Tuesday evenings, in San Francisco, were conducted the same as on Sunday, in Berkeley, everyone, including myself, called the Tuesday gatherings "meetings" and referred to those on Sunday as "church."

When I asked Master if we should call our Center a "Church" officially, he replied, "Call it an SRF Church as soon as you are meeting somewhere that will be permanent." It was Paramhansa's wish that we have our own church building.*

---

*The Bay Area members started an SRF Church Fund. We met in homes and rented halls until later, when after much searching, Edward and I located a church in nearby Richmond. The Self-Realization Fellowship approved the selection and it was purchased. This lovely chapel, Sunday-school rooms, other rooms and facilities, and ample parking, met the needs of our growing attendance. Situated on a two-acre site beside rolling hills, this quiet area is an ideal one for meditation and spiritual study. This has become the first SRF Church in northern California. It has been deeply gratifying to fulfill Master's wish to have a permanent place of worship here.

A number of members from our Bay Area SRF Center have formed Meditation Groups in their own homes, meeting regularly in various communities. It has been a source of satisfaction to all here, to see this expansion of our SRF work through these members. Several have gone from here, to Mt. Washington, to enter the SRF Renunciate Order.

Master thoughtfully arranged for my class notices and sermon topics to be printed at Headquarters. I included a wide range of his teachings, in which the Bible and Bhagavad-Gita were an integral part. Our Guru's wisdom lighted each subject with his insight.

Meditation
The Scientific Methods of Yoga
Help the Devotee Attain Oneness with the Infinite

Man has need for truths to make life understandable. He feels a need to see meaning in God's Plan for His children, and this comes into the scope of man's questioning. Sermons reach out to meet these needs, but they should above all teach the devotee to have personal contact with God in meditation.

When we turn to the sanctuary of inner silence, the restlessness of body and mind usually blocks our entry into this temple of quietness. Activity seems natural, whereas stillness is difficult to acquire. The concentration method taught by

Paramhansa Yogananda helps one achieve the relaxed state essential for interiorization of consciousness. The breath, interrelated with the mind, is never "held" but becomes quiet through this effective exercise.

The stilled mind is directed to God in the SRF Meditation technique through the Divine Manifestation of Vibration and Light. The Cosmic Om Sound (Holy Ghost) can be heard by practice. The inner Light may be seen by opening our vision within the "single eye." In sacred writings the "spherical eye" has been given many names, including "Third Eye," "Cave of Wisdom," and "Tunnel to Eternity." Within it shines the "Star of the East." The Light of the Star is the doorway to Spirit. Saints and sages of all ages have testified to the presence of Light in their experience of Cosmic Consciousness.

Kriya Initiation is given after one has studied the Praecepta lessons, which include the techniques mentioned. These basic techniques are prerequisites of Kriya and continue in regular practice after Kriya is received. These specific Yoga methods expand our capacity for Cosmic Experience in God.

One may be neither devotional nor religious to begin, yet the application of certain yoga practices can open the way to know God. The American College Dictionary defines Yoga as "The union of the human soul with the Universal Spirit."

Paramhansa Yogananda said: "Like any other science, Yoga is applicable to people of every clime and time. Yoga is a

method for restraining the natural turbulence of thoughts—
thoughts that otherwise impartially prevent all men, of all
lands, from glimpsing their true nature of Spirit. So long as
man possesses a mind with its restless thoughts, so long will
there be a universal need for Yoga."

CHAPTER 14

Sri Yukteswar's Prophetic Pronouncement

I often saw my Guru, although now living over 400 miles away. There were visits at Christmas and in summer. In addition, Master came north at times and drove to our home. Edward and I also visited with him in his rooms at the Palace Hotel in San Francisco when he was there. Later in the spring of 1950 I received this message from him:

"I am deeply pleased to hear from you and I am praying. God and Gurus are with you. Come in August if you can. I will visit with you then. My love and blessings to Edward and all at the San Francisco Center. God bless you."

His happy enthusiasm over the newly-acquired property in Pacific Palisades is expressed in his letter. I had not yet seen this lake setting.

June 30, 1950

Dear Kamala,

Are you planning to attend the Convocation—especially the *Lake Shrine* opening? You will be amazed to see this place. It is a paradise! Please write if you are coming.

People are coming by land, sea and air from every part of the world. These occasions will mark one of the great fulfillments of Lahiri Mahasaya's prophecy for my work— its gigantic expansion in 1950. *It is my wish that you can be here.*

With deepest prayers and blessings to you and Edward,

Paramhansa Yogananda

The following important letter arrived, which emphasized Master's special wish to talk with me.

August 8, 1950

Dear Kamala,

I had just written to you when I received your letter today. You must come this time. I have *some very deep reasons* for saying this which I cannot tell you now. I will talk to you at that time. This is my deepest request to you. At least come on the 20th for the grand opening of the Lake Shrine. Anxiously expecting to see you here. I must talk to you.

I am 14 hours a day busy editing 3000 pages of the Bhagavad-Gita.

All blessings to both,

Paramhansa Yogananda

The Lake Shrine is a place of rare beauty, as Master had written. It is located near the Pacific Ocean, on Sunset Boulevard. At the entrance is a Lotus Gate; inside the gateway is a large parking area and from here one may wander through rustic paths to the lake, which has already been glimpsed from the horseshoe curve of the highway above.

White swans glide upon the lake and in the waters are many fish.* Beside the lake stands an authentic Dutch windmill housing a lovely chapel. There is a Mississippi houseboat on the waters, and nearby is a museum containing interesting art objects.

On the grounds are statues of saints, nooks for meditation and contemplation, flowers and unusual trees from around the globe—a veritable haven for the horticulturist and all who love beauty and serenity in a peaceful setting. A life-size statue of Christ stands high above the lake, illuminated at night by a light focused upon it.

I was present for the special Lake Shrine opening. This day brought to everyone many hours in Master's presence. He dedicated the Gandhi Peace Shrine, into which he placed a portion of the Mahatma's ashes. These had been sent to Paramhansa, from India. All remaining ashes had been scattered over the Ganges. The Honorable Lt. Governor Goodwin

---

*Our Guru sometimes lifted a fish from the water with his hands and then returned it, after remarking how tame and unafraid it was.

Knight, of California, unveiled the large golden lotuses, resting upon a tall archway facing the lake.

The Lotus flower is used by the Self-Realization Fellowship on literature and in architecture. It is a symbol of spiritual significance in India. The opening petals suggest the spiritual unfoldment of the individual soul.

Master concluded the Lake Shrine Dedication with a stirring sermon. This talk and an account of these events have been described in the *SRF Magazine,* and movies that were taken that afternoon have captured Master's luminously beautiful expression and likeness with startling clarity.

Before the large gathering dispersed, Master acceded to numerous requests to autograph his books as many walked by to greet him and receive blessing. As I walked up to where he was sitting, near the lake, he referred enthusiastically to the beauty of the surroundings, and then added, "You will be at the Kriya ceremony." I nodded yes, pronamed, and went on, for although it was late in the day, a few people yet remained to see him.

The Kriya Initiation which Master gave at Mt. Washington included hundreds of students and culminated the eventful week of Convocation. I recall the lovely lei I carried as flower offering to the ceremony. Several had been brought from Hawaii by a member, delighting the Sisters and me. How beautiful they were!

As I went up to the altar the holy significance of the moment brought recollection of a previous Kriya that my Guru held there. When I stood before the Master on that day, he touched my forehead and prayed silently. Then he said, "God bless you. I am giving my blessing to you for the thousands you will initiate into Kriya Yoga." I had then walked on in amazement, returning to my place, unconscious of surroundings, deeply pondering his words. I still cannot express, adequately, the tremendous sense of responsibility they gave to me.

Master Finds Joy in the Flowers, 1950 Convocation

Following this present service, Master remained in the Chapel until midnight, receiving all who sought him. Among the students there were a few who wished to be shown the "Light" within the forehead, and he granted their wish as he placed his hands upon each in turn. This concluded the eventful evening.

I remained at Mt. Washington for twelve days and on the last day spent many hours with my Guru. This was an occasion when the atmosphere of his room was especially electric—charged and vibrant. It was a "live" silence with a dynamic spiritual force. I sensed Holy Beings present, including Master's dear self.

For a while my beloved Guru was withdrawn. Then he began to speak. As he talked there were occasional interruptions by a knock at his door. He would reply, make a decision or settle a question. He was attending to all matters brought to him but he was living more in a realm beyond this one.

These were hours in which he told me many things regarding his own life; some of them brought laughter with the telling; many were solemn and sacred to his innermost heart. I felt a sense of timelessness as he reflected upon the memories. Then, the moment arrived when he chose to convey this momentous news to me. He said:

"*Sri Yukteswar came to me* to tell me that *my time now is short*. I must finish what I have to do." He added, briefly, "He doesn't wish for me to talk about it."

Master would not add how long a time it might be. I remained several more hours in his blessed presence and then returned by train to Oakland.

Once alone, a grief that had been assuaged while with my Guru now shook me with force. I wept in untold sorrow through the long night, unseen in the sparsely occupied car. Yet in the days that followed I found that Master's dear and reassuring presence at Mt. Washington diminished my realization of his portentous news.

CHAPTER 15

Cherished Correspondence

IN earlier years I heard Master pray most often to the "Heavenly Father," yet it was with many Names that his heart called to the Creator—varying and beautiful Names suggesting our many relationships with the Infinite One. He also used poetic metaphors, movingly expressed, in his prayers and poems. Sometimes he addressed God in the feminine aspect of "Divine Mother," with Her Tenderness and comforting Love, and he has thus referred to God in some of his letters.

Master emphasized the importance of service. He spoke of it in many letters, as in this note sent to me in Oakland.

September 6, 1950

Dear Kamala,

God bless you both. Meditate deeply and regularly, doing everything within your power to carry on this great work of God. Keep the light of His love burning on the altar of your hearts, that it may light the way for others.

You are both ever with me. With all my love,

Paramhansa Yogananda

Paramhansaji tells of his preoccupation with his writings during a period of seclusion. His letter shows the loving encouragement he always gave to us.

September 22, 1950

Dear Kamala,

I am so happy to hear from you and appreciate your sending the check of royalties from your play "Ozma of Oz." Perhaps one day the Divine Mother will grant you the privilege to see one of the plays in production.* It was very thoughtful of you and Edward to send the check to me. I shall spend it for something for India which will remind me of you both.

I have retired from all outside activity and am spending as much time as possible with my writings.

It pleases me very much to know that you and Edward are doing such wonderful work there. Through your will-

---

*Master is referring to two children's plays that I dramatized from books by L. Frank Baum. They were published by Samuel French Inc. The royalties were from the yearly productions. In 1962, in Los Angeles, his words came true regarding my seeing a performance of one of the plays: "Ozma of Oz."

Sri Yukteswar and Paramhansa Yogananda in India, 1935.
Photograph made from statuette.

ing spirits these teachings will reach many God-thirsty souls. I am with you in Spirit and shall continue to be.

You and Edward are very dear to me. All my love and blessings to you both,

Paramhansa Yogananda

Edward and I were with Master during the holidays and his letter speaks of this visit.

January 12, 1951

Dear Kamala,

I was so happy to see you and Edward during your recent visit here. Thank you for your Christmas gifts and greetings. It was very sweet of you to remember me thus. I am delighted with having a statuette of my Master and appreciate the one you made of me.

God bless you both. Meditate deeply, love Him more and more, and join hands and hearts together in seeking Him within and without, everywhere.

It was a joy to see you. All my love and blessings to you both,

Paramhansa Yogananda

The statuettes he mentions were photographs on wood cut-outs. The one pictured here shows the two savants together in India, in the ochre robes of the Swami order. Master wrote saying, "Was so pleased to receive the additional box of statuettes from you and Edward. They are very good and I am delighted with them. The one of Sri Yukteswarji is very dear. I want to send some to India."

Several years later the other, of himself alone, was enlarged to life-size for the 1957 Convocation. This dear likeness, made from his picture shown on page 152, has been displayed at later Convocations, with his harmonium and other things he used.

One of my letters to Master had mentioned the efficient help given by members in the Bay Area. In his cherished reply he gives reassurance to all who continue steadfastly in their quest to realize God.

February 21, 1951

Dear Kamala,

It is good to have such workers, those who are wholeheartedly devoted to God and Gurus, and are willing to serve in order that the teachings will be disseminated everywhere. Through willing hearts, God can accomplish miracles.

Seek the Divine Mother with whole heart. Whatever time in life one begins the spiritual path, what matters is that one remains to the very end. Meditate with ever-increasing devotion. Then you shall receive the Divine reward: God-Realization.

I miss you both. With all love to both,

Paramhansa Yogananda

Master's great compassion for the peoples of the war-torn countries can be felt in this letter.

March 7, 1951

Dear Kamala,

I especially enjoyed your personal message, the essence of which I place at the feet of the Divine Mother.

Divine Mother has given me much work to do regarding the Korean situation. Many, many times I have felt the tremendous suffering now permeating that section of the world.

Trust you are well and happy. Anchor yourselves in the Divine by meditating deeply, morning and evening. Such is the way to establish permanent happiness in your lives.

With unceasing blessings,

Paramhansa Yogananda

As I re-read my Guru's letters, I think again of what they have conveyed through the years. In them I see his constant reminders of God. I see my Guru's encouragement, his blessings, his friendship. They have also said: Come to Mt. Washington, Come to the Religious Congress, Come to the Convocation, Come to the Christmas meditation, Come to talk with me.

It is the Eternal Call of the Guru to the disciple. Paramhansa has called me, as he has called to all—to realize God, and he has lit "candles of wisdom" along our way.

CHAPTER 16

Master's Harvest: Devotees of God

A wire sent on August 25, 1951 brought this invitation from Master: "Please come by plane or train for Initiation at 7 p.m. Saturday. Have expected you to come. Love to both, Paramhansa."

I attended the Convocation and after the week of scheduled activities was concluded Master sent one of the Sisters to ask how long I could remain. I had not come expecting to stay but replied that I could be there as long as Master wished.* She said he was leaving for Encinitas that evening and that I was to accompany him.

As we drove down the coast, a visiting SRF Center leader rode beside Master. In the car were also two Sisters of the SRF Order. It was a lovely drive and we soon arrived at the Hermitage, which is situated along the Coast Highway, overlooking the ocean. The beautiful building is surrounded by rich foliage. It was built when Master was in India, and he later dedicated it for an SRF Colony. Nearby on these grounds is a Cafe and an Inn where anyone may come to spend a

---

*I was privileged to remain for many weeks.

Paramhansaji at SRF Church, San Diego

period of time. In this restful place tensions seep out of one and allow the mind to become refreshed and more deeply attuned to God.

Our Guru has helped devotees prepare for spiritual plantings with the motor-plow of scientific Yoga methods. He said, "The disciples who steadfastly nurture the seeds of meditation will see them grow into a great tree of Realization, and others will then come to bask in the shade of their Peace." The many disciples throughout the world who loyally follow his precepts to know God are the Guru's Life Harvest. There were several of Paramhansa's most advanced disciples at Encinitas at that time.

Dr. M.W. Lewis,* the beloved presiding minister of this beautiful place, gave sermons regularly both here and at the San Diego Church. He was a disciple of Paramhansaji since 1920. He and his family lived in a home on the Hermitage grounds.

There were several SRF ministers then visiting at Encinitas. Some of them had come from distant places to attend the recent Convocation at Los Angeles. Among them was Mr. J. M. Cuaron, Center leader from Mexico City. This devoted disciple has translated Master's books and lessons into Spanish and has taught these precepts in Mexico and many countries in South America.

---

*Dr. Lewis became the vice-president of the Self-Realization Fellowship in 1952. The *SRF Magazine* for May 1960 gives a biographical account of his life as a disciple and minister.

Master gave special luncheons for the ministers, and one day while they were still gathered around the table he asked me to bring something to him, designating where I would find it. When I returned and handed it to him, he opened the small container, which held a precious True Relic that had belonged to Babaji. He showed it, reverently, to each one.

After many of the guests had departed, our Guru planned a picnic with Dr. and Mrs. Lewis, and I was included. It turned out to be a cool and windy day, but this did not deter him nor alter his enthusiasm, for Master loved picnics. He selected an area overlooking the ocean, located on the way to San Diego. Here the table was set up, folding chairs put up beside the parked car, and our meal was soon before us. We had to hold our plates from the wind as we ate the food that Mrs. Lewis had lovingly prepared, and we all happily shared Master's company.

Rajarsi Janakananda was also at Encinitas. This name was given by Master to Mr. James J. Lynn, a disciple who had achieved supreme Realization. He spent as much time at Encinitas as his business activities permitted. His advanced state of Consciousness was apparent; he radiated happiness to a degree that caused many to seek his blessing.* Someone said to me, "One can't describe it but you can feel the joy

---

*Rajarsi became president of the Self-Realization Fellowship in 1952. His life story appears in the March 1955 issue of the *SRF Magazine* dedicated to him and entitled: "The American who became an Illumined Yogi."

when he is near and see it in his face." Paramhansa once wrote of Rajarsi that he was "a Yogi of Himalayan hermitages of the past, who will light the lamp of Self-Realization in many groping hearts." This prediction has already come true.

I once heard Rajarsi say: "I follow this path because I am practical and *this is a practical path* which brings results. *It is not speculative.* Nowhere else could I find a way to achieve the spiritual realization I sought. The love and joy of God that I feel is without any end."

Through the years I noted that while others talked of truths—he meditated; that while others sought companionship—he dwelt in seclusion.

When Rajarsi came in to visit Master in the mornings, the Guru and his beloved disciple welcomed each other quietly. They discussed varied topics, and there were peaceful silences between them that were shared by those of us who were present. Those brief encounters left with me a picture of the great rapport which had existed between them for more than eighteen years.

Sister Gyanamata resided here at Encinitas Hermitage. Master has called her the greatest woman saint in the SRF. I can recall long ago at Mt. Washington her many duties and details to which she attended. Ever serving, she proved that a saint's life is not escape from responsibilities. None could prevail upon her to spare herself; she chose to act to the limit of her ability in serving God and Guru. In her room the words *"God Alone"* were placed to inspire her own moments there. They have also been an inspiration to others. Her *letters* to our Guru will be rewarding to any who read and ponder them, for holiness was her way of life. They are printed in many issues of the *SRF Magazine* and may one day appear in book form.

One of the many times when Sister Gyanamata was meditating and felt the vibrations of Master's presence bringing intense Joy, she wrote him that these spiritual blessings meant more to her than the wonder of vision.

Such wisdom! How many *saw* Christ when he lived who did not become disciples—but those who *felt* this Son of God within their hearts and souls became saints. Sister was making this comparison from her own experience, for she had many holy visions in her meditations.

When I first saw Master, in 1925, I wrote of his smile. She also mentions the beauty of his smiles in one of her letters. She wrote: "My ever blessed Master, I am told that records are being made of your voice, chanting. I wish that records could be made of the smiles that sometimes flash on your face in response to some secret emotion. The smile you gave me lately was as truly a blessing as a touch of your hand on my head. So God smiles on me through you. Gyanamata."

Her name means "Mother of Wisdom." It was given to her by Master at the time she took her renunciate vows to become a Sister. All of the disciples found her a truly wise

Mother. Our Guru left Mt. Washington in her care while he was away in India.

Distance proved to be no barrier for his blessings to reach her. When he was abroad she wrote, "I had the great happiness of feeling the uplifting vibrations of your presence. They grew stronger as the day passed and at my meditation I floated in a sea of peace and joy."

In another letter to Master she told her revered Guru, "Each time I marvel at the joy and well-being that comes to me when you draw near in Spirit."

I was visiting with Sister Gyanamata for a little while in her room at the Hermitage before our return to Los Angeles. As I rose to go she asked if I would carry a message to Master, to ask him if he would look up at her window, from the car, as we drove out on our way to Mt. Washington that day. I inquired if she wished to have him come to see her before he left. She assured me she wanted only this. How few would ask so little! Sister knew her Guru would respond to any wish she made.

My reminder caused Master to stop the car in the grounds. Looking up, one saw her God-consecrated face there, sweetly waiting. He looked long, then lifted his hand in a parting blessing and we drove on. She was at that time near the closing chapter of her life.

CHAPTER 17

A Montage of Work, Wisdom, and Humor

UPON our return to Mt. Washington the days were filled with many duties for Paramhansaji and he worked almost around the clock. Disciples alternated to keep pace with these activities. It was known that our Guru rarely slept more than two or three hours in twenty-four. Even so, that would be assuming he slept in each of those hours when alone. Disciples returning for a memorandum only moments after they had left his rooms found him already deeply absorbed in meditation.

We also could observe that in the few times he lapsed into the even, regular breathing of sound sleep, he was continually conscious, and if our low-voiced conversation brought up a question in which he could help us, he would open his eyes, his breathing change, and answer whatever we had been pondering. Sleep did not bring unconsciousness to him!

There was never formality in the coming and going of disciples to attend to duties or receive instructions. Some came in regard to office matters; they had letters for Master to answer and took dictation. His suggestions were required concerning the forthcoming issues of the magazine and the publication of books. His advice was sought on a wide range of matters. Once a disciple remarked to me: "It doesn't matter how a problem appears to need a certain kind of solution, if Master directs the very opposite it always comes out right, and afterward you can see where any other way would not have worked out as well."

Often Master talked to us in the late evening, sitting by the open windows. Once, when he was reminiscing about his life in India, he recalled, with a chuckle, a childhood memory and related the story to us. It concerned his music lessons, which kept him from play, so he did not welcome the regular visit of the teacher, who was soon to arrive. On this particular day, entirely without such intent, he put an end to his coming. Young Mukunda, (Paramhansa's given name), re-marked to his sister, "When he comes he will have ——— coins in his pockets." He named the exact sum of money. His sister, unbelieving, gleefully told the teacher, expecting to show her brother's statement to be a product of his imagi-nation! The teacher listened and took the contents from his pockets. He saw exactly what the small boy had declared. Then Mukunda named details regarding other objects and he began to verify these too. As each statement was proven, the poor professor grew pallid. He suddenly dropped them all and fled from the house, never to return!

Questioned by his Father, the boy admitted this unusual behavior and further added that he would recite word for word from any book opened in some other room while he remained where he stood, blindfolded. His proposal was accepted. His Father put a blindfold on him, chose a book and page at random in an adjoining room, and heard him call out accurately a recital of the entire page. The Father realized this to be amazing but when the boy concluded, his wise parent told him not to repeat such performances, which were all too startling to the beholder.

Through the tall tree-tops the night sky was azure and summer sounds were present in the air. But our minds were still in India where Master's story had taken us, and a disciple brought up a question regarding a certain yogi who used to walk under the water on the bottom of a deep-flowing river. Paramhansaji answered her, then very simply said to me, "I can do that too." I nodded. It is conclusive that one who can control heartbeat and breath can also remain underwater.

Master has said, "I could walk on fire and fill every auditorium with curiosity-seekers, but what good would that do? See the stars and clouds and the ocean; see the mist on the grass. What miracles compare to these? People need to know the love of God."

Our Guru always showed us by example and teaching that absorption in God is the reason for our being and that nothing less can satisfy us for long.

I have heard both disciples and visitors speak of sensing a Power in Paramhansaji. He possessed a dynamic force that was evident even when he sat quietly absorbed in some work. I have seen it in his eyes, sometimes, and it acquainted me with the reality of power and dominion of a kind the mind cannot fully grasp. Always reined with gentleness, it could be intuitively felt.

A disciple asked Paramhansaji about the presence of God in Creation, manifested within its varied forms, and about the pattern of change and evolution. Master instantly gave her question his entire attention and explained with detailed answers, profound and specific. It was often in this informal manner that disciples received his teaching.

Master remarked, "The disciples who are around me are not 'Yes' people; they all have strong wills." Some of them had been renunciates for twenty or more years at that time; others had come more recently. They had a quietness in common and came, not with talking and problems, but to serve in God's work. One day a Sister left the room after receiving some office instructions from Master. He said to me, "I have been training her all these years. . . . Now I am satisfied." I knew he was commenting upon the role she would play in future SRF work, for steadfast discipleship was fitting disciples for the responsibilities later assigned to them.*
His comment made me cognizant that the time was near when he would be placing the work in hands other than his own.

*One of the Sisters became president of the Self-Realization Fellowship in 1955.

One evening Rajarsi phoned from Encinitas. Master told me to remain in the room. I believe he wished me to hear his words to this beloved disciple. He told Rajarsi, "You have pleased me in every way; you have fulfilled my every wish for you." Words for a disciple to treasure!

Master was intensely interested in world affairs and listened each evening to the ten o'clock news broadcast. We always dialed the news for him at that hour, whether in the car or at Mt. Washington.

One young student often used a gift of mimicry so amusing she could bring instant laughter by making a 'face,' and one could hardly resist the feeling of hilarity from her comic antics. Master told her to be more grave. She obeyed and when she changed her ways I noted her stature and loveliness increase as dignity replaced the clowning ways.

Master always knew how to guide the disciple to elicit the best and to help him or her grow better. Luther Burbank (noted horticulturist who practiced Master's teachings, including Kriya) showed with plants that only by blending them with a new life could stubborn "fixed" habits and deep-rooted tendencies be changed. The plant then sets out on a new way, never again to return to the old. This is an apt comparison of the Guru's guiding hand in the life of a disciple.

The suggestions and counsel of a Master can undoubtedly help the disciple to bypass much unhappiness and lessen life's difficulties if he is alertly responsive to heed the helpful direction. But I found our Guru's guidance was never imposed, never forced, and often very subtly given. He did not impose even a wise and best way, because he gave freedom of will and choice. Sometimes he would remain silent on a point, in contrast to his happy, positive attitude when all was well.

One instance of this, in my own life, concerned a time when my Guru gave me an unusual blessing which he said would continue throughout my life. At the same time he enjoined me not to do a certain thing. Since this was a usual kind of activity that was to apply to me, I thought that it might, at times, be necessary, so I asked if I could make exceptions. He looked away and then said yes, but was averse to give his consent. I should have realized it was not best, because he was always so happily enthusiastic about anything he knew to be right. I made this exception soon after, and certain adversity resulted. The benefits I thought needed were entirely lost! I finally saw how he had tried to guide me although I had not grasped the full import of his wise counsel. Since then I have never made exceptions. The special blessing has remained with me.

Sometimes I wished to retain some of the prayers our Guru spoke during the evening meditation. I wrote down what I could remember, then asked him for help. Whenever I did, he was always able to recall his words, and this seemed remarkable to me because his prayers were spontaneous and varied. But he felt deeply whatever he prayed and his devotional thoughts were etched in his consciousness.

One of the many endearing qualities of our Guru was his appreciation of the humorous side of life. I walked into the room one day and found him reading the comic strips of Blondie and Dagwood, and Maggie and Jiggs. It was enjoyable to be present because these marital explosions and domestic perplexities were bringing forth his chuckles and soon even his shoulders shook with his laughter.

Master always relished the dénouement of a true story about a man and wife he knew many years ago. The wife nagged her husband constantly about everything. It was embarrassing to everyone but was so ever-present that the husband seemed not aware of it. Paramhansaji counseled her to change the habit which sounded so discordant. She accepted this good advice and withheld all tendency to speak in that manner. Delighted with the result, Master commented to the husband about her wonderful change. The husband admitted it was true she had changed entirely, and that it must be more peaceful for their friends. Then very sheepishly he confessed: "But you know, I rather miss it!" Master's hearty, infectious laughter joined our own when he came to this unexpected conclusion in his narration.

I believe our Guru was in sympathetic agreement with many men in regard to some fashions in women's hats. I recall a day, long before, when I stepped into the car wearing a new hat. It was made up of a few flowers at the top of the head. I saw that he was bubbling over with a mirth he found hard to contain and which increased the oftener he happened to glance at it. At that time hats were not little dots on top. They were head coverings! Master always seemed to like my sense of appreciating humor, but I had regretted my choice of an advance style too much to fully enjoy this—although I have in retrospect! That which stays in my mind was his reference to it, some 18 years later, when we were again driving, and he said, with sparkling fun in his eyes, "Remember that hat?"

One Christmas Master gave me a lovely printing of "The Hound of Heaven" by Francis Thompson. On long-past occasions I had heard him give part of it on the lecture platform. Now, in his room, sitting by him quietly, I referred to this poem he loved. His face lit up, and to my delight, as I had hoped, he began to repeat the immortal lines which picture God ever-pursuing while we run from Him. Wisdom garbed in poetic beauty! The majestic cadenced words again stirred me as I listened to his spirited recital of it.

I was present when Paramhansa gave the following suggestion to a devotee in regard to her child. He said, "She has a very strong will, and will not accept too tight a rein, so do not tie her too tightly in your dealings with her, and guide her without letting her feel the pull of it. Give her room to move. I see her life clearly before me."

A number of the SRF Sisters enter their vocation while quite young. Their early and sustained attraction for this way of spiritual service could be an indication of some past training—perhaps of a former life in such an environment. In one instance Master confirmed this when he said that one of the young disciples had been a Mother Superior in a convent in a former incarnation. Rarely, however, did my Guru reveal such things.

A Master will never disclose anything without an inner prompting from God. At those times he sometimes commented, "God has let me tell you this," or he might explain gently, "God will not let me say."

Many years ago Master told me that when we first met he had recognized me at once, from the past. Later he mentioned a past association, briefly conveying his part and my own, but never referred to it again. His comment brought to mind how the Guru continues to be with his disciples life after life.

Early tendencies and impressions had suggested certain settings to me, such as my occasional surprise in childhood when I looked in a mirror and expected to see my face reflected, but of another nationality. I was also a vegetarian from birth. Although meat was served daily at our table, I was not made to partake of it. I wondered, fleetingly, from these and other reactions, where I had lived in a recent incarnation. I asked Master, yet I am surprised I did so, knowing a Guru will tell you when he wishes you to know. I found him reluctant to speak, and he looked away, yet in kindness he named a country as a general answer. This corroborated much I had felt and I asked for a specific location. He replied, still more reluctantly, with a name that thrilled me: Brindaban—place of pilgrimage—birthplace of the great Avatar, Krishna. However, Master's brevity forbade further questions. I realized, even more deeply, that he wished my attention to be focused upon the soul's unchanging identity with Spirit. He always emphasized our lineage from God rather than our earthly incarnations, since our spiritual heritage is to be found through remembrance of the unchanging Eternal Self.

One morning our Guru spoke of going back to India. I was totally unprepared for my sudden outbreak of tears when he mentioned this. But I knew instantly that if he went on this trip, I would not see him again. However, it was not destined that he return to the soil hallowed by his Guru and Paramgurus.

Early in Master's life he was given a preview of two pathways, and the privilege to decide which of them he would take. He recounted to us that he was given a choice for a meditative life near the River Ganges, without any suffering, or to go to America to give spiritual guidance to countless thousands, yet endure physical suffering near the end of his life. His decision was for our benefit, and for the many in the future who will find their way to God through his teachings.

One day Master glanced at me and asked, "Do you have all of my letters?" This was his first and only reference to the letters which he had written to me through the years. His gaze was steadfast, waiting my reply. His question had not been asked casually but rather spoken with emphasis, and I replied, "Yes, everything you ever gave me." His nod of approval expressed satisfaction. It was when I recalled his question, long afterward, I realized it had been formulated with foresight that I would be writing this book.

CHAPTER 18

Privileged Hours with My Guru

THOSE autumn days at the Fellowship continued to be busy ones. I marveled at Master's miraculous power to handle all the details, great and small, in the course of a day. The welfare of the renunciates and of members everywhere was his concern, and visitors came from all over the world to see him. He was busy from early each day, with hours of work already completed when I entered his rooms. I would be seated while he finished whatever he was concentrating upon. Shortly he would look up to greet me with a "Good morning." I would "pronam"—greeting in the Hindu manner with hands touching one's forehead; outwardly serious, serenity in my heart.

An atmosphere of calmness pervaded his daily relations with everyone. His unfailing sweet courtesy, and his thoughtfulness and inner repose, made the days conducive to thoughts of God during one's activities.

It may seem that one would have many questions to ask a Master if privileged to be with him. But I found that when I was with my Guru I was lifted into his atmosphere of peace, and other matters were resolved or forgotten. This was true at my first meeting with him, and whenever in his presence.

I felt blessed to know that Master wanted me with him; that he had sent for me to come. It was ever an unspoken wish to be with my Guru, and it gave me special happiness to be able to serve. To be with him was a privilege, and it always brought an inner sense of divine contentment.

India has long recognized the spiritual blessings received in the environment of a Guru. Once Master humbly conveyed this thought, after I had completed some small service for him. He said softly, "Perhaps you will receive some benefit, too."

There were services which I was able to fulfill, but I knew that Master called his disciples to be near him, not for what we could do for him, but for what he would do for us.

Interwoven with Master's great calmness was a sustained vitality that had no dependence upon sleep. I never saw him in any kind of a letdown feeling that comes to almost everyone. In all of those weeks, as in the previous years, he never appeared weary, even after full days of 12 to 19 hours, filled with the many matters that come to a leader of a large organization, and the spiritual counseling that was sought through many letters and personal interviews. I observed that this all-too-human frailty did not touch him. He had tremendous reserves of energy and power that can only be described as "from God."

He once touched his forehead and then said to me, "When I put my thought here I do not feel the body at all."

In an instant he could be absorbed in the Infinite to the exclusion of all else. He was thus beyond the need of techniques and yet, as an example and help for all of us, he meditated with us and never missed doing the recharging exercises both morning and night. Late at night he would step out on the open porch, close by his suite of rooms, to do them. I would often accompany him.

Master was generally writing or dictating during the hours after midnight; often the many letters and occasional cablegrams to India were composed during this time which was free from interruption. Whenever possible, he turned his attention to the books he planned to complete, furthering them at every opportunity. He usually wrote them in longhand. These were typed by secretaries. Sometimes he made small inserts on his original script or on the typed copy.

Before we (the disciples) went to our own rooms at night, we meditated with him and he always directed us to practice Kriya before we concluded. We remained quietly absorbed for a time, then he would say "God bless you" and "Well, good night," or "You may go now." These words were spoken with a kind of gentleness that always gave the feeling that he shared your regret that the day had ended and the hour had brought its conclusion. Yet one never felt dismissed—only very sleepy at times and glad that you would be again with Master on the morrow.

Paramhansaji liked to go out for a drive in the evening before his writings would again occupy him. Sometimes we would have dinner at a Drive-in where we were served on trays in the car. Once we drove up the coast as far as Oxnard and we all went into a restaurant with our Guru, where we enjoyed a meal of Chinese cooking.

One evening, driving in the Pasadena environs he saw a home with a second-story verandah in a setting of tall leafy trees and shrubs. He said with enthusiasm, "Look! That is the most like a home in India of any house we have passed." The car was stopped while we saw the home that had brought to him a picture of the loved land of his birth, and doubtless he flew there in nostalgic thought.

A conversation with Master that began most casually when out on one of the evening drives proved to be a forecast of a happening that would transpire shortly afterward. He had been speaking about the coming Christmas meditation. Musing, I said I hoped our car would bring us. (The previous year it had burnt out a main bearing while en route and we had missed the occasion of the 23rd, although we were there for Christmas.) He nodded thoughtfully, saying, "You need another car; what kind should it be?" His question was a rhetorical one and he was quiet a few moments; then he told me, "You should have a Chrysler."

I did not grasp the import of his remark while I replied, agreeing that we should consider the buying of another car. He spoke no further about it. His way was not to portend foresight; he presented it very simply as a suggestion. How humble he was! possessing wisdom of which he made no show.

Four months later in Oakland, the concluding part of this account took place when Edward answered the phone on January 16th. One of his brothers was calling to ask if he would like to have his car because he had surprised his family with a new one. Edward said, "Yes, very much, for we cannot depend upon our own." He spoke about arranging payment. His brother replied that it would be one dollar for the transfer and not to protest, because if he insisted upon paying more he would give it to someone else! So the car—a very good one—came as a gift. Yes, it was a Chrysler!

On the occasions we left early enough to be out in daylight hours, Master would have food brought along on the drives. This was carried in a container with many plastic compartments wherein were placed several kinds of fruits and nuts, and a large thermos jug held fruit juice. Fresh limeade was a favorite with all. Master gave an individual blessing whenever he placed a serving upon each one's plate and directed it to a disciple or guest. It was not to be passed on to someone else. This personal kind of blessing always accompanied anything that he gave: a flower, fruit, or any gift.

In a lecture Master once spoke of spiritual qualities that are present in foods. He said the body exists to manifest the soul and that every food has certain inherent qualities. We benefit from these different magnetic vibrations. To illustrate, cherries have the vibration of joy. Bananas, a very spiritual food, impart calmness and humbleness. Enthusiasm and fresh energy are derived from eggs and milk. Oranges and lemons banish melancholia and are a brain stimulant. Almonds and honey each reflect self-control. Berries aid clearness of thought. The strawberry is attuned to dignity and grapes have special vibrations of Divine love.*

Master was inventive in creating unusually delicious recipes. One of them combines pineapple juice and fresh parsley—a drink made in a blender and served very cold. It is green, refreshing as mint, and healthful.

Calcutta croquettes are another example of Paramhansaji's ingenious culinary art. He found all of us willing samplers and tasters during the various testings of his new recipe, which became popular at the SRF Cafe in Hollywood. Another favorite on the menu was the "mushroomburger." The cafe offered a wide variety of East Indian food, all vegetarian. This found favor with many people in the community as well

---

*This is a partial list from my notes taken in 1925. I did not ever hear him repeat this talk or see the list in print. The other foods he mentioned appear in the second printing of *Priceless Precepts*.

as SRF members from this and distant areas. It was always exceedingly busy. Another SRF cafe, located at the Hermitage in Encinitas, prepared the same special foods. Renunciates served, wearing the graceful sari-dress of India. Some Brothers of the Order were also occupied with duties connected with the cafe. A lecture hall adjoined the restaurant, and many Church activities and Convocation classes were held there.

When Master drove to the SRF Cafe, the disciples were overjoyed at the unexpected visit from their Guru and came out to group around his open car door and windows. Those of us who had been riding with him left the car to make room for the others while he talked with them. Master liked to remain out of doors on those beautiful summer evenings.

Edward drove south when his work permitted. He was also studying for an advanced academic degree. On an occasion when he was there, our Guru invited him to go on the nightly drive. We stopped at a restaurant along the way, where we all shared the evening meal together. Edward felt the blessing and privilege of being with him during those hours.

On one of the drives along the coast Master spoke to me about the value of SRF Colonies. He referred to the forming of groups within a city or a rural area in the manner of hermitage life, among members who do not desire to be-

Edward, at the Time He Received His Degree

His untiring service at our SRF Center
in northern California for twenty-five years
includes many years as a Service Reader.

come renunciates, or cannot do so because of certain obligations. Such a life would enable each one to be in daily association with those who share the same spiritual goal. He described such Colonies as made up of married couples and their families, as well as single people, who have the will to serve, and to live in harmony with one another. Master envisioned the idea as one in which all may work together in a self-supporting group wherein each one is dedicated to God.

A drive to the Lake Shrine one night allowed our Guru to talk to the SRF minister there. Those of us with him went into the lovely Chapel by the lake until he was ready to leave. When we returned to Mt. Washington there was an instantaneous gathering of the men disciples, who had been on the alert for his coming. This always took place whenever he returned, whatever the hour. We would go in while he remained talking with them. Those hours in his company were eagerly awaited, and valued indeed, by each one.

He guided devotees so that outer form and ritual would never replace inner realization. The Master said, "It is not what you wear but what you are inside that matters. Make your heart a hermitage and your robe the love of God." He said, "I would like to feel that the light of devotion for God I have lit in your hearts will be eternal."

Those words, and other remembered conversations with Master, were jotted down by some of the disciples, both men and women, and this valued material became the book entitled *The Master Said*. In this volume Paramhansaji seems to be here, again speaking directly to us. What would he tell us? What would he answer to a question we would like to ask today? Often his reply is before us in this book. His wisdom touches upon the many aspects of human experiences and how to view them, and of our problems and how to meet them. The reader may feel he is in the company of this enlightened Master, receiving his wise counsel. A disciple will find his Guru especially close through these sayings which give light on the highway to the Infinite.

One Sunday evening two renunciate Sisters and I accompanied Master on a drive to Manhattan Beach. As we neared the ocean, on a road bordered by tall eucalyptus trees, he wished the car to be stopped. Enough daylight remained to see the wide expanse of the water. Master was quiet for a little while and when he finally spoke his mood was reminiscent. He recalled our lifetime of discipleship, and commented upon our being with him "in the beginning, and now at the ending." His words, spoken so simply and without emphasis, poignantly reminded me that but little time remained before he would be gone. In Spirit there is neither beginning nor ending, but earthly life does begin and terminate.

CHAPTER 19

My Guru Enters the Great Samadhi

UPON my return to Oakland I received several letters from my Guru. He wrote, "Trust all is progressing regarding the Center meetings." I had resumed our regular services, and the special pre-Christmas Meditation was planned. In January I was giving a Kriya Initiation, and a class series of the basic meditation techniques in February and March.

Master continued with his writings. He loved the beauty of the desert and sometimes wrote at the SRF tree-shaded bungalow in Twentynine Palms. He refers to this place in his next letter. He also speaks of finances. This concerned the buying of a Church he wished for the Bay Area. He said to me, "We need a hive there for the honey of God."

At his request we looked for a Church but had not yet located a suitable one. The Church Building Fund for this purpose is mentioned in Chapter 13. It was his wish to have a permanent place for worship here, and he had told us of his plans to help finance it.

November 13, 1951

Dear Kamala,

I have your letter of October 19th and remembered you and the group on the evening of the 23rd. I would have replied sooner but have been away, enjoying the desert air for a while. Expect to return there sometime this week. Am busy as usual with the phone ringing constantly.

My heart is light because I am again working on my books. Was up until the early hours of this morning writing. I am working on "Genesis" and extremely busy. It will be a great relief to complete a few more books and I expect to keep at this while at the desert.

Please write about your plans of spreading the work. How is it going? I am raising finances for you. [This was for his help in the purchase of a church when we located one.]

Try to come at Christmas. Can you? On the 23rd is meditation, on the 25th, 2 p.m. is dinner. You are both invited.

Ever yours, with love to both,

Paramhansa Yogananda

Paramhansa's thoughts about our Center, and his reply to a prayer request, are in his next letter.

December 15, 1951

Dear Kamala,

I am very happy to hear from you and to learn briefly of the progress of the work there. I was pleased to read the good news about the home which has been offered for the Berkeley meetings which are to commence in the New Year.

It was interesting to note that you are having a Candlelight Christmas Devotional Service at the San Francisco Center tomorrow evening, and my thoughts will be there with you.

I received your letter regarding Mrs. ———, and I immediately began praying for her. Please keep me informed about her condition, and tell her to keep her faith steady, and to pray, deeply and often, "Father, I am protected in the castle of Thy Omnipresence."

I am glad you and Edward are both coming for Christmas. I hope to be able to talk with you more in detail at that time when I see you. Please let me know when you are coming and how long you will be able to stay.

Until then, all my love to you both,

Paramhansa Yogananda

We were at Mt. Washington for the holiday season. The pre-Christmas, all-day meditation was spent in prayer, chanting, and silent worship, with hearts attuned to Christ. Paramhansaji meditated with us. He spoke of Jesus and his Oneness with the Father, of his living Presence, and of how Christ may be born again, within our consciousness. This special Christmas service which highlights the Holy Season is held in SRF Churches and Centers throughout the world, and is uplifting for all who participate. I have attended these meditations at Mt. Washington as many times as possible during my lifetime.

Christmas day Master sent word for us to come to his rooms, where Edward and I visited with him and received his thoughtful gifts. When we were seated at the dinner table I took notes on the talk he gave in order to carry his message back to our members in northern California, and I thought again of the privilege that was ours to be in the company of one whose life has exemplified the Precepts of Christ.

Master asked me to come on the following day to see him. At this time Edward visited with the Monks. He knew many of them and always spent time with the renunciate Brothers when he came to Mt. Washington.

Christmas, 1951, with Master. Facing left to right, Mrs. Lewis, Rajarsi, Master, Dr. Lewis, a guest, Kamala, and Edward. Many disciples were present to share the blessing of this memorable occasion.

While I was with Master we meditated together for a little while; then he talked to me of many things, especially concerning SRF activities. Time passed all too quickly. When the hour to leave had arrived, Master asked for Edward and then gave each of us a blessing. Reluctantly we departed, with pronams of respect and devotion.

I was not to see my Guru again! But I did not know this as I received his parting blessing. How overwhelmingly sad and shocked I would have been if I had but realized it. With all of his words preparing one, a veil seemed to screen my actual comprehension.

When again in Oakland, I had a great longing to talk with Master. Although so recently with him, my mind was strangely demanding. It was as if my sense of urgency was an intuitive prompting, for while I was not then aware of it, this was to be the last time I would hear his voice while he was in his earthly form. I called long-distance in the early hours of January 5th. It was his birthday. While we visited he asked if I could return for awhile. I mentioned the Kriya Initiation in January and the Class Series that followed at the Berkeley Center. Those already scheduled plans blocked my perception of his expressed wish. I was later to learn, when my Guru was no longer here, that I had missed a last precious opportunity to be with him. This brought an aftermath of remorse. My oversight assailed me with sudden force. It was like seeing in focus what had not previously registered. Such lessons, taught through the pain of regret, are well learned!

Paramhansa was invited by the Consul General at San Francisco to attend the India Independence Day celebration there. Master wrote and asked that we represent him on this occasion.

January 17, 1952

Dear Kamala and Edward,

I was very happy to see you both at Christmas time. I missed you at the birthday party on the 5th.

Please write me often with details regarding your Center work, though I am unable to write you regularly due to lack of time. I hope everything you have planned is proving successful. I send my kind thoughts to both of you all the time.

I have received a letter from the Consul General about joining with the celebration in San Francisco for the India Independence Day. I am busy getting the book ready for publication so I will be unable to attend. I have written to Mr. Ahuja today that since I am unable to attend the function myself, I am sending my representatives, you and Edward, to represent me. Please convey to both the Consul and his wife love and greetings.

The enclosed card will give you the details of the celebration ceremony.

With my love and unceasing blessings to you and
    Edward,

                    Paramhansa Yogananda

We attended the reception, which was given on that occasion by Mr. and Mrs. Ahuja at their home in San Francisco. The Consul General, and the Ambassador from India, were planning to visit Master very soon. My Guru writes of this in his last letter to me.

February 20, 1952

Dear Kamala,

I was happy to receive your letter of January 26 telling me about the reception for India Independence.

I have been snowed under with work on the book, and have been unable to take care of the letters that have arrived. The book is progressing very nicely, and I hope it won't be too long before it is ready for publication. I am working day and night toward that end.

The Indian Ambassador to the U.S. is arriving in Los Angeles for a visit in March. *I am planning to attend the reception at the Biltmore* for him. He is coming to see me at Mt. Washington and will also visit the SRF Cafe and the Lake Shrine with Mr. Ahuja.

I have been so busy writing on "Genesis" and international mail, I have been overwhelmed. But I was most happy—as always—to hear from you. Please write definitely what I can do. Do write me no matter how busy I am.

With all my love and blessings to you and Edward,

Paramhansa Yogananda

Paramhansaji's expected guests visited him at Mt. Washington in March. They went to the SRF Cafe and to the Lake Shrine. Each plan Master mentioned in his letter was carried out, including the reception at the Biltmore Hotel on March 7th, in honor of the Ambassador from India.

This was the same hotel where my Guru had stayed when he first came to Los Angeles in 1925. Twenty-seven years later, in 1952, Master was again at the Biltmore Hotel, but this time it would be the scene of his Mahasamadhi.*

Paramhansa Yogananda addressed the banquet guests on that evening. Just before he was called upon to speak, he turned to one sitting beside him and said, "Always remember: life has its beautiful roses and also its thorns; and we must accept both."

In his talk he spoke of the need for God in the world. He described the ideal combination: the activity of the West and the meditative qualities of the East. In concluding, he quoted from his poem "My India." At the moment he had spoken the last words of the poem, he slipped from his earthly form.

My Guru, my dearest friend in life, was gone. I was stunned with the inevitable shock of the news. He had escaped into the vast Infinite, but I knew only an emptiness. I had the sad

---

*Maha = great; samadhi = bliss; a realized soul's final departure from the body. At that hour God granted a wish Master had expressed: that when he die it would be while "speaking of God and India."

Paramhansa Yogananda—Revered Preceptor

Picture taken one hour before his Mahasamadhi
at 1952 banquet honoring the ambassador from India.

duty of informing the class in Berkeley, where I imparted his teachings. I told of Master's passing, barely concluding before tears of grief took hold, a grief that silently filled the hearts of everyone.

On March 17th I held a special Memorial Service in San Francisco. A large gathering of people from all parts of northern California came to offer homage in his honor.

Master's series of Bible interpretations of the words of Christ had been appearing in each issue of the *SRF Magazine*. I can recall the startled feeling that came to me when I saw that his writing in that current issue for March 1952 was entitled *"The Final Experience."* It was from Luke 23:46 that he had selected the text: "Father, into Thy hands I commend my spirit, and having said thus, he gave up the ghost."

A student told me that Master had remarked to her that he would remain in the world until finishing his books. When a recent letter from him informed her that he had completed his books, she did not grasp the significance of his words. Later, it had seemed so evident! There were many such instances.

Emerson said in his essay "Spiritual Laws" that "we cannot see things that stare us in the face until the hour arrives; then we behold them and the time we saw them not is like a dream."

There is some comfort in the words of Master when he wrote similarly of his own Guru, Sri Yukteswar, while visiting India in 1936. "Basking day by day in the sunshine of my Guru's love, unspoken but keenly felt, I banished from my conscious mind the various hints he had given of his approaching passing."

My mind went back to the year of 1933 when Paramhansa Yogananda had taken several of us with him to Forest Lawn Memorial Park in Glendale. Together we walked through its halls. We passed towering Michelangelo replicas, looked at the stained-glass window of "The Last Supper," heard the melodic strains of "Ah! Sweet Mystery of Life," and went by many sunlit alcoves. Soon, his dear body that had served the Heavenly Father so completely and without reservation would be taken there, to reside in a crypt called the "Sanctuary of Golden Slumber." I feel he knew of this future event even as we walked there.

The Los Angeles newspapers were soon to carry unexpected headlines that said Paramhansa Yogananda's body was in a state of non-decay, of immutability. The perfect preservation would become a phenomenon unparalleled in mortuary history. It would be discovered at the Forest Lawn Mortuary while the coffin remained unsealed for twenty days awaiting the arrival of disciples from India.

It seemed a long drive from Oakland to Los Angeles on March 11th, because it was a sorrowful one to be coming to the Services where Paramhansaji's loved form lay in the Chapel at Mt. Washington.

It was a very silent gathering although many hundreds were present. There was no overt demonstration except for tears which fell silently down the faces of many. Some of Master's favorite songs were played on the organ. They included "Battle Hymn of the Republic," "Ave Maria," "Ah! Sweet Mystery of Life," and "The Blue Danube." Rajarsi Janakananda and Dr. Lewis conducted the combined Christian and Vedic rites, and India's Ambassador, His Excellency Binay R. Sen, expressed India's homage to Paramhansa Yogananda in his eulogy—a warm, heart-felt tribute that also revealed the personal esteem he felt. The Honorable Mulk Raj Ahuja was also present. His endearing words about Paramhansaji appear in the Memorial issue of the *SRF Magazine*. This special issue also includes the tribute of Ambassador Sen and it gives a record of that day and events preceding it.

Throughout the service I felt Master's *living Presence*. I could not see him but what I felt was so actual, so real, that grief was lessened during those hours. After the hundreds of people passed by to view his peaceful countenance, they left to return to a world less bright. The resident disciples remained in the Chapel singing many chants.

My saddest moments were when the casket was being slowly carried from the Chapel, through the foyer, and away from this home that was his. All of the devotees were chanting the ceremonial Rose Chant. We had each gone to behold Master's dearly loved face, and from baskets of rose petals took some to scatter before him as his body was taken to the waiting car. I felt great bereavement witnessing this departure which gave such finality to his passing.

In those hours, and the days following, I knew the aloneness that is caused by that great sense of separation ever-present when a dear one has passed on. Yet a Master, dwelling in Light, can span this inscrutable barrier at will. My heart and mind believed this truth. Very soon I was to have confirmation of it.

CHAPTER 20

My Guru Brings Dulcet Reminders of God

PARAMHANSA YOGANANDA said, "Whether I am in the body or not, I shall stoop down from heaven to make those that will be in tune realize the love of my Father."

This promise he has kept; this blessing I have received. Because he has slipped from a loved form does not mean that he is beyond reach. Realization of this has come unsought. I have been cognizant of my Guru many times. His holy vibrant presence has been variously manifest to me. In every instance I have found exactly the same spiritual benediction as when he was here in his earthly body.

A Guru with Cosmic Consciousness is not "there" or "here" but rather, he continues to be One in the Cosmos. I wish to express as clearly as possible that the relationship with such a one is not "contact with the beyond" but an ever-continuing one with a "living" Guru who was able to say, "Unknown I walk by your side and guard you with invisible arms."

Paramhansa Yogananda wrote in his autobiography: "The consciousness of a perfected yogi is effortlessly identified not with a narrow body, but with the universal structure. . . . He who knows himself as the omnipresent Spirit is subject no longer to the rigidities of a body in time and space."

Paramhansaji came to awaken love for God. All of his spiritual Reminders continue to open doors of soul receptivity. St. Paul said: "Eye hath not seen, nor ear heard . . . the things which God hath prepared for them that love Him."

When my Guru has made his presence felt it has always been to bring me from my own immediate state of consciousness *up* to one as high as I am capable of experiencing. This differs from time to time. Sacred Joy the Guru can impart as we are able to receive. When sense of ego, body, and possessions is forgotten, then the devotee may feel identity with Spirit.

In each Touch of God we feel the fulfillment of all longings, and in these perfect moments we are lifted into a Divine Happiness. We are affected more deeply, more tangibly, than by the material world of the five senses. It is never a state of excitement; but rather, a degree of quietude that we seldom know at other times. It fills us with longing to dwell constantly in this Happiness of God.

Eighteen days after my Guru's Mahasamadhi I recorded the joyous notation that Master appeared to me.

Master here—seeing him so clearly! He came into the room and *blessed me* and *spoke to me*. I remained quiet in his loved presence, in the wondrous contentment it brought me. Later, in my morning meditation, the fragrance of unseen *roses* pervaded my room when I began Kriya.

A few days later my Guru was again visible to me, bringing indescribable comfort. I wrote of it in this diary entry.

Master came! Here in my room suddenly *Master was standing right before me.* He was not only dear to my sight but so tangibly here that impulsively I reached forward to put my hand on his arm. He looked at me, said gently, "Well. . . ." Then he began to vanish. I wanted to ask him to stay longer but he was gone. I believe my movement broke the stillness needed for me to see him.

At the 1952 Summer Convocation while I listened to a letter from India being read, about Master, there were such forceful currents in my spine I could not absorb them all. The intensity of the Pranic energy brought blissfulness; tears filled my eyes. This came through Master's Blessing; I felt his uplifting presence.

When soul blessings come, they so inspiringly affect one that the question is often asked, "Is this something that others have also known? Is this a part of our going to God?" I have always cherished these hours within the seclusion of my heart and soul, unspoken, until now when I write of them through Guru-given sanction. My ministry among people sincerely seeking God has taught me that many wish to evaluate their inner realizations without disclosing these sacred happenings. Our Guru has given enlightening guidelines to us regarding the spiritual states of consciousness in the holy experiences on our pathway.

Blessings from Paramhansaji have come to me in many ways since his passing. Some of them are described in the following notes written after 1952.

Holy Fragrances

I awoke early and sat up to meditate. I sensed my Guru was here. His presence imparted Peace. I also noticed a sweet floral fragrance. When I went into an adjoining room, the air there was also filled with the same scent of flowers. Sometimes God gives these lovely fragrances; sometimes my Guru does so, ever reminding me of God.

★ ★ ★ ★

While typing this evening, the scent of *gardenia* was present, as if flowers were there beside me and everywhere in the room—very redolent. An hour later, when Edward came in, I asked him if he could smell any odor. He replied, "Gardenias. Where are they?" He went outside but found that no flowers were in bloom. Then he asked, "Is it an astral fragrance?" And so it was.

* * * *

In the quiet of meditation I felt Master was here in the room. A little while afterward, while I was busy putting household things in order, I placed my copy of *Whispers from Eternity* on the rail of the balcony. I became aware of the aroma of *roses* emanating from his book of prayer and filling the air around it. This remained for a long while.

* * * *

When Edward and I visited an SRF member in the hospital, I took a picture of Master with me. I opened my handbag to take it out and noted the sweet odor of gardenia. I did not have perfume or flowers with me, and she had none that gave any fragrance. Then as I handed his picture to her, the *fragrance was everywhere* in the room. She took the picture in her hands, eagerly and lovingly, and looked at it with great reverence. Both she and Edward spoke of the gardenia scent. Afterward, on the way home I opened my purse several times and we could inhale the sweetness coming from the picture. When his picture was again placed in my room, the area was permeated with the flower scent.

Protection

This summer I have especially desired Master's blessing for the coming vacation trip. A vision of impending tragedy has caused me to delay our departure long after we have been ready to leave. Then, this evening while I was talking on a long-distance call, I suddenly felt my Guru's presence here in the room. I asked my friend in Colorado to please wait, and in those moments following, the assurance and blessing was given; the special protection that I had asked was granted.

What occurred on the trip came very close to what I had seen in preview; it touched, yet was averted! A strong karmic condition was present and some tremendous suffering was in store, but not the greater disaster I had witnessed in vision because of the Divine intercession of my God-attuned Guru.

Prayer

I have been pondering a certain difficulty and wondering what to do. My mind has returned to it frequently. Today when awakening from a short nap I *saw Master* before me, in side view, his hands together in prayer position. I felt his message was for me to *pray:* to meditate and pray more. After his clearly viewed face faded from my waking sight, he again appeared before me. Each time he was visible to my open eyes. I remained quiet, realizing that he had come to show me that prayer would bring my answer from God.

Prayer Response

In times of mental, physical, or emotional problems, we seek the help of greater wisdom and power than our own. There is always an answer that resolves our problems in a Divine way if we can go deeply enough in prayer, and sometimes we need to persist through long periods of time.

From a seemingly unending karmic problem, I knew the weary desperation of fruitless search for an answer. I sought to find a way to change that which would not change. It swept like a tidal wave over the emotions and gave actual physical pain to the heart. My greatest protestation of the problem was its power to disturb my mind from God. This caused me to turn to God with fervent prayer.

There were three times that followed, during this great trial, when *God responded* to my long, deep, continuous *prayer* by suddenly *lifting* me so above and apart from specific grief that there was surcease of all sorrow. These were instances when I felt completely *within the still, infinite place of being* where God's Presence Alone exists. Instead of a solution to my problem, I realized that *this was the answer,* the solution. Not by changing circumstances or problems but by God's very Presence.

Nothing could disturb that Peace which lasted long enough each time to bring changes within myself. Often "answered prayer" comes in this manner. Problems are not always changed; we are. We can act and not be acted upon; not be depressed nor shattered by the circumstance. Until this occurs, how vulnerable we are! Our own particular Achilles heel is exposed to barbs and arrows that affect us, and take us from our Center of Peace in God.

Sometimes, in rare instances, guidance has come to me from God or Guru in words that were audibly voiced. Three of these times are recounted here.

****

While I was praying for the wisdom needed to choose between two diverse paths open to me, God spoke through my mind. This sentence came with great clarity: "Do nothing until the answer comes." I realize now that Patience is the answer, rather than action, at this time. (How often, when perplexed, we want to act immediately! Yet God knows when conditions are right for us.)

****

Tonight I prayed with deepest urgency and concern. I needed help in facing a serious problem. What should I do? Master replied! In the still night I heard his words, spoken audibly, and recognized his voice. My course of action was concisely given. (Good results followed his unusual advice that was both disciplinary and rewarding.)

* * * *

I sought my Guru's will in regard to an important decision concerning my SRF activities. I prayed for his thoughts to guide me. Master's response came in a way I had not anticipated; he spoke to me. In his words he gave me detailed direction—wise and far-seeing.

Conscious Sleep State

Paramhansa Yogananda wrote: "I attuned my life with Thine and now . . . Thy Fountain of Bliss intoxicates me night and day in my *wakeful states, dreams* or *hours of deep sleep.*" Master has here indicated his awareness of Bliss in each of these states.

When a true Soul Experience takes place in sleep we may become cognizant of such an occurrence in one of two ways. (1) We either *recall* what has already taken place, after waking, or, (2) we are *conscious* of such happenings *while they transpire.* On the occasions that I have experienced the second way, I go to sleep naturally and then become aware, but without thought of the physical body, which continues sleeping. I am conscious of what is happening as it occurs. It takes place in the *present* and I *participate*, thinkingly. I need not waken afterward (being already conscious) but simply open my eyes to see my immediate surroundings.

In sleep the life energy (prana) is partially withdrawn into the spine and brain from the sensory and motor nerves, leaving the body completely relaxed. It is therefore an ideal time for spiritual receptivity if one is consciously aware.

In soul perceptions during sleep, the experiences may take place in an earthly, or an astral, setting. Sometimes all form is forgotten in Spirit.

Instances of *conscious sleep* since Paramhansaji's passing are presented here from my diary notes.

Holy Communion from Master

I became conscious during sleep and was standing at the door of a large room where many disciples were present. I recognized many of them. Master was presiding at this gathering. He was seated on a quite low platform. I entered the room and one of the Sisters led me up to him. His gaze rested upon me, and I saw he held a communion wafer. I knelt and my Guru placed the wafer in my mouth.* I could feel it on my tongue. He then took my hand in both of his, saying, "This will tingle a little"—and a *cur-*

---

*Communion wafers are not used in our SRF Services, but my Guru did so in this instance.

rent went from his hands into mine and I could feel it travel up my arm and directly to my heart. By concentrating I could hold it there, or rather, keep aware of its gently permeating force. After the blessing imparted in these vibrations, and through the symbolic wafer, he asked me to repeat these words: *"Saints Always."* This I did. Then I was again in my room and still suffused with the sacred blessing.

I have found the words "Saints Always" have great power to bless one through the train of reverent thought they invoke. When dwelt upon, the mind is filled with the sublime ones who walk with God.

Darshan

In the night I saw Master walking up a hill, in his robe of orange, and many people were following a few feet back of him. The scene was one to give *upliftment.* It is the blessing that is given through sight of a Holy One, called darshan. I continued to stand, from a distance, viewing the scene and feeling the *inner glow* that it bestowed.

Attunement

I grew aware during sleep and saw Master walking toward me across a green lawn. As he drew near there was the sound of music, to which we both listened. When this ceased we sat on the grass to meditate and remained in complete silence for a long time. I felt perfect attunement with my Guru. His presence imparted an *infinite Peace* which pervaded me. It was truly the Peace of God. When Master rose and walked a few steps away, I saw he was as a youth in appearance, as a man of twenty, yet Master just the same. Only this and one other time did he appear so. And the Divine Peace has remained with me throughout this day.

Wisdom Symbolically Given

Evening. I felt tremendous need to sleep in a very different way than being sleepy. It was as if being drawn into it. When I closed my eyes for sleep, I was *with Master* seemingly at once and intensely aware. It was an outdoor setting much like a picnic area. Many others were there, including Edward. Master took Edward and me to a separate table where we were seated. He gave us many presents, and as he presented each gift I felt his great love, and my own overwhelming gratitude. I was not aware of the contents of any package; they were expressing, rather, his *spiritual* giving encompassing all of the years. I thought: "How much you have given me of the Eternal things." Then he indicated that we were to go far up a road where we would again be with him. We went down an incline to reach the road. Edward continued to walk on, but I paused there, momentarily, looking up at Master. He was on the edge of the dirt embankment about 12 feet above. With a cane he moved a small stone, but it seemed to loosen and dislodge another one, the size of a football, and his expression was one of great concern as the large stone came forcefully down toward me. I couldn't tell where it might hit! I felt a strong air current as it moved past me.

I said to Master, "I couldn't tell which way to move, so I stood still." He replied very gravely: *"Yes, sometimes that is also God's way."*

I feel this is a lesson he wished to convey—a truth, too, so he pretended concern but only so I would feel it real and respond naturally. But I had no fear. So wonderful to be with Master!

This experience just related came to have a tremendous meaning in my life, portending a great karmic blow, the natural effect of a cause in my pathway. Master saw it would be loosened upon me at a not-too-distant time. When it came I wanted with all my being to move, to act, to do something, but the Divine inner guidance of God and Guru continued to be the same for me that I had experienced in this vision: to "stand still."

A Vision of Rajarsi

In a sunny and peaceful outdoor setting I was sitting beside Rajarsi. We were talking about a certain kind of spiritual blessing. As he spoke I saw a look of inner ecstasy come upon his face, and there was a tone of wonder in his voice when he said, "I recall spending a whole night in meditation, feeling that rapture!" I thought: How *deeply* a saint tastes the Wine of God! Later in the same vision I saw him again, among a group of people, teaching. He moved from one to another, giving spiritual counsel and blessing. I noted his great calmness. I believe Master wished for me to see Rajarsi on the Other Side, serving others as he had served on earth.

A Precious Visit

Early this morning Master came and stayed long, talking of many things. I was aware, so aware, but the body was sleeping. Afterward, I felt a sweetness in my heart from his presence, and thought of all he had said to me in this wondrous time of communication.

Space Journey

I became aware during sleep and found myself beside Master's Guru, *Sri Yukteswar*, traveling in space, seeing *vast vistas*. The wonderful feeling is hard to describe. So free from any limitation of movement! Sri Yukteswarji was beside me just as two people might walk down a path together. But we were moving with arrow swiftness! I knew he was enabling me to do this, guiding me, for it lasted an incredibly long time. During that period I could see the treetops of forests, mountains and valleys—scenery I love. We spanned both greens in summer warmth and landscapes with the white snow-covering of winter. We were high above the earth, and ever-present was the feeling of *space*. My mind was quiet as we moved. This flight, unimpeded by gravitational restriction, gave a sense of great freedom.

Loving Solicitude

In conscious sleep I was with Master. We had been walking and conversing for quite a while when we came to a building resembling a country club. We crossed the wide porch and entered the front door. I saw it was furnished informally like a mountain lodge, and present here was a group of SRF members gathered for some special function. They paid no attention to us as we came in, and continued their activities of building a fire in the fireplace, and preparing a meal in an adjoining kitchen. Now we were sitting nearby, but when Master talked to me no one turned in the direction of his voice, and then I realized that they did not see us at all, because they were in some earthly setting and we were then in astral form. Master and I were quietly waiting. I knew we were there because Dr. Lewis had just passed on, and Master was staying with this little group until word came through regular channels to inform everyone there. I thought how often our beloved Guru may be present in times of sadness or rejoicing, though we may not know it.

Occurrences in Dreams

When happenings transpire during sleep and are recalled *after* waking, in retrospect, we think of them as dreams. There are many kinds of dreams, including those from the sub-conscious mind, which do not impart special joy.

Paramhansaji said, "Practice of the Hong-Sau (concentration) technique will save you from years of fruitless wandering on the *sub*-conscious plane. That is the land you want to avoid; it is full of illusory or imaginative experience. One must realize the *Super*-conscious state to have real spiritual experiences and realizations of truth."

When a true Spiritual Occurrence takes place in a dream—
an experience that stems from the Super-conscious (Soul)
state—it can be recognized as such by the glow of Happiness
and Serenity that is felt when the dream is recollected after
waking.

Five dreams of this kind are presented here.

****

I awoke today recalling a dream with Master. We had
been standing in the center of a large room talking for a
time when, with decisive movement, he turned to go over
to a chair where he sat down and became absorbed in
meditation. I sat down and closed my eyes. At once I saw,
with inner sight, a fire of tall flames beginning at the base
of my spine and rising to my shoulders. I could feel it,
also, as vibration. It was of "light" not "heat," and I felt
joyous. I sensed Master wished me to raise (lift) the flame
into the Christ Center.

****

I was with Master and Sri Yukteswarji in the same way
one is with one's family. It was so natural that I had no
thought of the wonder of it until I wakened recollecting
the treasured hours. I felt a divine Peacefulness that is still
with me.

* * * *

Blessed dream! A treasured time with Master. I was in a pine-tree setting and heard Master call me. When I came near he asked me for a drink of water. He stood beside the entrance of a rustic building. I went inside and filled a glass which I took to him. He drank it slowly and seemed to relish it. He looked at me and said thoughtfully, "It has just the right taste" and I saw he was pleased. Then I knew a tremendous soul happiness and realized that he had called me in order to impart this sacred joy to me.

* * * *

Awoke this morning remembering a clear dream of being with Daya Mata. She was in lotus posture on the floor, holding an object in her hand which we discussed, spiritual in import. I sensed about her a great tranquility— a lightness of being—and my thought, after waking, was of her being within a pool of *tranquility*. It was inspiring to feel this quality radiating from her.

A Master's Kindness

Lahiri Mahasaya's only available photograph does not reveal his eyes, although one senses their spiritual radiance. At times, through the years, the wish has come that I could see their expression. It was but a whisper of a thought. Yet this morning he granted my wish in a dream. I was in a room with a few people. In a leisurely way we conversed as we went to a long table where we seated ourselves. Master and Lahiri Mahasaya were there. I was explaining something to someone near me when I stopped speaking in the middle of a sentence, thinking: "Why am I talking of non-important things, with these two Great Ones present? Master is here! Lahiri Mahasaya is here!" And as I thought this, Lahiri Mahasaya turned to look at me. He had the merriest expression, and I received his thought which told me, "I am granting your wish!" As I looked intently, solemnly memorizing his face in full view, he continued to hold my gaze with his eyes that sparkled with smiling warmth. In those satisfying moments he seemed to understand my gratitude. He continued to smile and give me all the time I wished to imprint his eyes and their expression indelibly in my memory. I was completely aware, and an inner serenity pervaded me. Then I was again asleep. When I wakened I thought of the immense kindness of this great Master to fulfill my wish.

* * * *

Blessings

I have found that Divine Blessings are conveyed with equal sacredness and potency through any one of the three states: Conscious Sleep, Dream, and Awake. These states have been described and designated only to identify. The following are in the "Awake" state.

Radiance

Today when I began to meditate, the room about me was entirely filled with a blue radiance. I felt bathed in the *blessings of Christ*.

Light

Early this morning I awoke looking into a scene in the Christ Center (Single Eye). This was a *garden in Light* and *of* Light, for flowers, trellis, grass, everything was illumined from within its very atoms, as shining Radiance, in color. The loveliness of it! I know that everything in essence is pure light; here God showed me light *in* and through *form*. I tried to go further into the garden and my efforts caused the scene to vanish.

The Star

In meditation the *Star of Light* was before me, large and perfect, surrounded by intense blue. I was completely Still in the wondrous *Silence of God*.

Expanded Vision

I sat up to meditate and an inner vision came. Within a deep blue color, surrounded by golden light, was a complete view of a nearby mountain and all of the surroundings. All of this vast area was clearly before me, in perfect detail, just as a telephoto lens would give. And this cinerama, with its great distances, was encompassed within my forehead. These outer scenes appear so lovely, viewed by inner sight!

Spherical Eye

After our SRF class tonight, when talking to a student, the inner Light appeared unexpectedly before my open eyes in the brightly-lit room. It remained. I closed my eyes a moment and it was also before my inner sight. The eyelids, open or closed, had no effect upon my seeing the Light before me. Wonderful to perceive during activity.

Love

God's Love encompassed my heart today at the all-day Christmas meditation. I felt the *warmth* of His Love exactly as if a mirror had caught the sun's rays and directed them upon my heart, which glowed with a pure Christ Love of immeasurable depth.

Spiritual Flower

In the spiritual eye, within the silver star, appeared a *rose* of perfect beauty. As I looked at it, the velvety petals began slowly to open before me, requiring several minutes. From almost a bud it unfolded to full-bloom perfection. It was large, life-size, and so close, as seen within my forehead. I knew an *eternal Stillness* which I felt then and for long afterward. Everything vanished from my mind except the Rose and the Stillness as I gazed at its living perfection.

The Holy Ghost

The descent of the Holy Ghost is described in the Bible in Acts 2:2, when the disciples were all together: "Suddenly there came a sound from heaven as of a rushing, mighty wind." This is the great Cosmic Sound called *Om* in Hindu scriptures.

When I received the Om Meditation from my Guru in 1925, I could not hear this Cosmic sound. I heard other significant inner vibrations but not the Om.* Many were present who lifted hands to signify they heard it, but I was among those who took longer. Perhaps I made too intensive an effort, for relaxation is a key to meditation. Later on, practice brought results! Finally I could hear it during meditation, and it also became audible whenever I was in quiet surroundings, but it still escaped me during any physical activity, or in noisy environment. After coming to the Bay Area I was very active as a minister with SRF work. One of the great blessings from God and Guru came to me at this time, when the Om Vibration one day filled my ears with its blessed sound, and my body with its vibration. From that moment it has remained with me as strongly audible during activity as in quiet meditation.

At times the ever-present Om Sound increases in *volume*, as if it were a roaring wind, or the hum of a giant motor in a power plant. And it pours through the body as Vibration as well as sound. Low in pitch, it does not ever pulsate. It is without beginning or ending—truly of God! I treasure this Divine Sound with thanksgiving.

*Except in times of special blessing, as mentioned in chapter 9.

Joy

I was looking at the beauty of the sunrise when I felt the *electrifying* tingling in the spine, and a Joyousness. I was cognizant of Master's presence. He stayed just a few minutes. That *Joy* has been with me ever since! It can only be described as a singing, dancing feeling of Spirit.

Friendship

Today when I awoke, *Master appeared* before me. I opened my eyes and he was here. The gaze of his calm, luminous eyes was deep. As he looked at me, seeing far into my soul, I sensed his holy mindfulness of me. He did not speak, and stayed but briefly. Yet those quiet moments imparted a deep Contentment to me. I felt the solacing touch of his divine Friendship.

Holy Visit

Tonight the mountain cabin was *aglow* with *Guru* and *Paramgurus*. The air was *charged* with their Radiance. When this sublime blessing touched me I became absorbed in ineffable happiness, imparted by their presence.

One morning after meditation I opened the pages of Master's *Autobiography* and these words leapt to my sight: "When your book is finished I shall pay you a visit." It caught my breath! In that instant I had an inner assurance that the words were, at that moment, a message of promise in my life. This proved to be true. With the conclusion of these writings the two following occurrences came with torrential blessings, and each brought fulfillment of that promise.

Babaji Comes

Babaji blessed me! I am so filled with this sacred happening that I cannot write fully of it yet. The remembrance of his presence beside me, and the divine blessing he gave to me, have brought gratitude and a feeling of awe.

Mirror of God

A tremendous experience! Master bestowed the Bliss state upon me! It began with an afternoon nap that turned into conscious sleep, and then continued after I wakened. I saw a large crowd of people walking up a road, and as I observed them I knew, suddenly, with complete certainty, that Master was about to pass by. At that moment they paused, and there among them was my Guru. He stood looking directly at me with a smile of Infinite sweetness. The people near him were not aware of his presence, so seemingly absorbed in reaching some destination. I

Tall Trees Planted by Paramhansa Yogananda
Portray Winter Beauty

thought: I can have the blessing of walking beside him if I hurry to reach him. Everyone, including Master, now moved on, very rapidly. I called out that I was coming to join him. I reached him, breathless from my efforts. Then I turned to look again into his dearly familiar face. At that instant everything vanished—all form melted from my sight. Pure *Bliss* engulfed me. I was conscious only of Bliss. I was awake, Divinely awake! The Om was resounding and I knew perfect Rapture in Spirit.

Looking into my Guru's face, I had found the Formless Cosmic Bliss! Afterward, I thought with reverent wonder how the Flawless Mirror of my Guru reflects God.

Paramhansa Yogananda sent this beautiful message on his greeting card one Christmas:

The whole ocean of joy rolls beneath the little wave of your consciousness. Do not be satisfied with a little silence. Go on endlessly. It requires pursuit of day and night meditation to get results.

The happiness which God gives is greater than anything the world can offer. Divine Joy is eternal. When everything else melts away, that Joy remains.

If you would experience this Joy, spend more of your time in Solitude. Remember that real happiness is found in communing with God in meditation.

Although you meditate two or three hours at night, and then sing and talk to Him, at first you will find no response. Then, suddenly a Light will appear. Suddenly a Fragrance will come. This is the way God manifests Himself to man, but it requires great persistence on your part.

Just behind your eyes, just behind your thoughts, just behind your feelings, is God. When you are calm, the whole universe of Happiness rocks beneath your consciousness.

That is God speaking to you.

Paramhansa Yogananda, Poet, Sage

CHAPTER 21

Poems by Paramhansa Yogananda

A Brief Description of Samadhi

Unseen Fetters

I Found I Was Everything

The Guru Calls His Disciples

The Dream of Eternity

My Guru often composed poetry when I did not have
paper or pencil at hand; finding them as quickly as possible I
recorded his words, sometimes at Mt. Washington, sometimes in a rural setting or near the sea. The inspiring poems
presented here are from my notes. This is the first time they
have appeared in print.

A Brief Description of Samadhi

by Paramhansa Yogananda

There was no swimmer.
There was nobody to look upon that Sea.
There was nothing but the Sea—
    the Sea of Cosmic Bliss.
I was that!

Touches, aromas—all vanished.
Stars melted, the earth melted—
    both vanished.
I perceived the Cosmic Sea of Bliss
    without the waves
    of Creation.

Unseen Fetters

by Paramhansa Yogananda

You may roam about the world with your feet unbound by chains. You may wander with your hands unfettered. You may move about the world in seeming freedom. You may perform anything your fancy dictates. Yet, are you free? Are you unfettered?

There are unseen fetters stronger than chains: golden fetters, iron fetters of good and bad habits that bind you. If you roam free, in seeming freedom, bound by cords of ungovernable whims and uncontrolled passion fetters, you are bound by iron fetters of dark habits, by golden chains of desires. If these bind you, you are living in the present house of the senses, working out their terms.

The cords of mortal instincts, though unseen and invisible, are stronger than iron chains to bind. When iron chains bind you, others can break them for you. But your chains are stronger still, entangled chains of habits. Others cannot break them for you, nor even you, by your momentary strongest determination. Yet, it is you, only, who can break your unseen chains.

I am my own judge; I serve my own sentence, dictated by my own karma. I forge my own fetters; I mold my own prison house; I break my own prison bars. I melt them into nothingness by my own efforts. I weave the garland of my laurels of victories and reward myself and wear them. I throw the garland on my neck myself.

I build the walls of many prisons around myself, by myself. Since I make my own fetters, and bind them around the free feet of my will and actions, shall I remain bound, or shall I break my chains and forge fetters no more?

I reward myself; I punish myself; I am the judge of my own destiny. Since God gave me reason, God is not responsible for me. He gave me free choice to make my own prison or make my heaven here. He gave me power to judge; so I am the judge.

Death comes by mortal command of fear. It shall go by my immortal command of deathlessness and fearlessness. Since I am a prisoner trapped in my own prison, unfree from my own sentence, what shall I do?

I may forge fetters around my feet; I may erect a million prison houses and sentence myself for a million transgressions; but still I never can imprison my free reason, the freedom of my will, the wish to be good to myself. Even the most lowly one, the most cruel of all, the most evil of all evil-doers is kind to himself, is good to himself. There is that desire for freedom, for upliftment, for racing back to the heavenly house. So we never can suffer perennial banishment, perpetual imprisonment. Hence everyone is free.

I am a man living in a prison house of habits and pre-natal instincts, bound by the chains of ever-increasing self-perpetuating chains of living desire. Yet free!

I shall break my own chains! I shall work out my own sentence. I shall shorten my term as I desire. Even as God is Master of the Cosmic House, of this Cosmic Kingdom, so am I, being His son.

He is free! I am free! I dreamt I bound chains around my feet. I am awake. Lo! my feet are free; the brain-born chains vanished. I am free again!

I Found I Was Everything

by Paramhansa Yogananda

My Soul, like a ball of transparent cloud, like a ball of dim grey cloud, shot into the bowl of the sky, whirled, burst in ever-increasing circles until it spread and disappeared and melted in the sky.

Once in a while I would see myself as different from the sky, as ocean and as the sunlight on the hill. And quite often, from the sky, see myself sitting on the hill, in my body, breathing, watching the sunlight.

But most of the time I would feel that the little ball of cloud (my Soul) had disappeared in the sky and transformed itself into the heaving ocean, into the vast sky, into the scorching rays of the sun and condensed piece of earth, and the little body sitting on it.

Many a time I would find myself as a little body, and many a time I would see myself as the ocean, as the sky, as the sunlight, as everything. Many a time I wondered whether I was the body, or the scenery around it. Many a time I put a million eyes into the scenery, and through them watched my body apart from it.

But at last, through the two eyes in my body and the millions of eyes in space which I had fixed around me, I saw with One Eye, One Vision of my Soul. And I knew and realized my ignorant separation, and found myself in *all*. I found I *was Everything!* Even as He is!

An ecstatic Joy came in the calmness of my Soul.

The Guru Calls His Disciples
by Paramhansa Yogananda

I am moving on. Come on, my own, my all—let's go!

Whether on the barge of life or drowned beneath the waves

of life and death, or sunk beneath the sea of Eternity,

we shall yet be on the bosom of our Mother Divine.

She calls us through all nature. I cannot stop. Come all!

Or if none come—I shall go.

The Dream of Eternity
by Paramhansa Yogananda

Life may be a dream, or
    Life may be real.
But if it is a dream,
    and I the dreamer,
    the dream unreal may be
      But I am real,
      I know!
Eternity gleams through me!
    Thou art real, for I am.
      I know!

I stand on the island
    of the Present.
Around me lies the mystery sea
    of past and future life.
I am alone—yet
    crowded with a million thoughts,
        with a million experiences
merging from the dim past;
crowded with a million premonitions,
    vaguely seen
in the story-house of future life.

Is the Present real,
    while the Past, which once
    seemed so real is but
        a forgotten dream?
I see that by tomorrow,
    Today will be a dream.
I see that again all
    the tomorrows will by and by
    say good-by to me.

Is the Past real?
    Is the Present real?
        Is the Future real?

Is it reality or unreality?
Is the ocean real
        and the waves unreal?
Yet—the waves sleep secretly
        on the bosom of the sea.
How can I forget the Past?
    Or the Present?
            And the Future?
They all lie buried
        beneath the Cosmic Sea.

I want to see all those I saw,
            and with them
I want to take all
        those that I love, and all
        that I am yet to know,
On my little raft of Eternity.

I am headed for the heavenly shore.
    I mind not the storms
            of Mystery Changes
            that sweep on Life's sea.
My joy is in my wish to go, and to take
    many others, to
    My Father's Home.

with unceasing blessings
Paramhansa Yogananda

The Flawless Mirror and *Priceless Precepts,*
books by Kamala, disciple of Paramhansa Yogananda.
Distributed by Crystal Clarity, Publishers
14618 Tyler Foote Road, Nevada City, CA 95959
1-800-424-1055